The Tao of Parenting:
The Path to
Peaceful Parenting

Lisa M. Smith, M.S., Msc.D., Ph.D.

Sealofters Press, Inc.

1061 East Indiantown Rd, Suite #104

Jupiter, FL 33477

Sealofters Press, Inc. was established in 2008 as a publishing alternative to the large, commercial publishing houses currently dominating the book publishing industry. Sealofters Press, Inc. is committed to publishing works of educational, cultural and community value.

To Stephanie, Kevin, Alexis, Kent & Riley –

You are my greatest teachers.

The following interpretation of the Tao, modified for the topic of parenting was derived from several translations of the Tao te Ching.

Invitation to Meander

Having worked with the original work by Lao-tzu, Tao Te Ching (translated The Book of the Way) for many years, it has become integrated into my way of being. I find it beautifully applicable in parenting as it is all about finding the balance in life. I know in my 24 years of meandering down the path of parenting my 5 children, "balance" has been the peaceful place I have surrendered to over the years. But it has taken daily practice, trust and surrender.

The Tao teaches us that we know ourselves through our extremes and boy, are there extremes in parenting! Angela Schwindt says, "While we try to teach our children all about life, our children teach us what life is all about". A life well lived and peaceful is lived in balance. Parenting through the Tao Te Ching provides age-old wisdom and guidance for Peaceful and Conscious parenting. It is what I like to call Parenting On Purpose. We are no longer parenting our children unconsciously (as in – the way we were parented), but are mindful of how we show up.

May your path be peaceful and purposeful and filled with much love, laughter and joy!

In love, light, abundant blessings & gleeful giggles,

Lisa

1

When you don't have an agenda, when you are not looking for what you want to create, you are open to what wants to come. From the same "Darkness" come all things if we are willing to sit in the dark and wait for understanding.

Darkness is "Source" to me. If our lives play out on a stage, Darkness is the ever–present "no-thing-ness" or backdrop to the stage our lives play out upon. "The curtain" (in this scenario) would be our awareness.

When we parent, we have the opportunity to peer out from behind the curtain and view what is "playing out" on the stage of our lives. Yet, often, we are so center-stage of our lives, that little time is spent behind the curtain. As we begin to view these "characters" (known as our children) that we have perfectly cast in our lives (and they, us), we can ask ourselves, "What is the role I have cast them in?" and "What is the role their soul wishes to play?" And, "Does the role I am currently playing facilitate this?"

As the "drama coach" in their lives, I have the opportunity to help them learn, grow and it is a continual balance of helping them with their lines while also allowing them to tap into their innate talent and allowing them to shine in their own ways. As a parent, I can become aware of my own drama as it is playing out and be certain I am not entangling my story with my child's.

When issues arise, I can stop, take a deep breath and become the "awareness" to what is happening – the "as-it-is-ness" and ask, "What is this about?" Who (me or my child) should be taking responsibility for the "lines" and how can I support and coach my child so that they learn how to respond to similar situations that arise in their lives without my continual prompting?

When in "Dark", remember, it is the birthing place of all things. The light within will be lit when we open the curtain (our awareness) to what is happening. "Free from desire" – as in, we allow what is happening to happen without resistance.

When we do this, the lights go on, the stage is lit up and the "stars" of the show shine in their own light, own awareness and can live out their own stories to thunderous applause.

Curtain call anyone?

2

When we choose sides we separate from one another and we can separate from parts of ourselves. If something is labeled "beautiful" then there is something that we can label as "ugly". When we have an expectation of what is "good", then we have immediately created something that is "bad".

These are all constructs we create within our own selves. Everything just "is". When we label something our child has done (behavior) as good or bad, we have not created a situation from which they can learn. We have boxed them and ourselves into a no-win situation. We all get to know ourselves through our extremes, which is in turn how we find balance. Children are no different. They bump around trying to find out "what works" and what doesn't work. We forget that this is what life is all about. Behavior ("good and bad") is a language. It "speaks" as to how the child is assimilating and relating to their world. When we label it, we take the learning out of it.

As masters in parenting (and we all are!), we can act without doing. This does not mean that we sit passively by as things fall part (or seem to in our every-racing minds). All actions arise from a state of consciousness that is grounded, connected and fully present. It is like an archer right before they release the bow. They see only one thing and that is the target. Clear. Present. Alert. Aware. A master parent, "teaches without saying anything" – our very presence – our "being-ness" is the teacher. "Things come and go and she allows it" – this is the essence of being at peace with what is happening.

While in Ohio, my daughter was stung by a bee. I heard her cries from inside and it was as if nothing existed in my world, as I "honed" in on her. I flew like lightening to her, whisked her up and had iced it and applied baking soda within seconds. It was this single-focused, linear-laser like action that arose from a clear, calm state, yet ignited what needed to be done. What was "to do" was not even a question. It happened through me.

What does this look like at bedtime with a child that refuses to sleep? Linear-laser: We get very clear about what is important. "Does my child really need to do this?" In this case, yes. We tell our child that although we cannot "make" them sleep, we will provide the opportunity to do so. We then give them a choice of "lying here quietly and sleeping" or "lying here quietly." There is no struggle, no "good or bad", only opportunities to learn how to be in this world, assimilate

4

information, and experiences and grow. In the end, we do not "make" anyone do anything. We simply offer opportunities to learn and experience and hold a space that is clear, aware, unshakeable and unconditionally loving.

We stop labeling and we begin loving.

3

"Practice not doing and everything will work out."

"Not doing" is an uncommon practice in Western society and in particular a foreign concept in parenting. The list of "to do's" as a parent is endless. I'm sure the concept of "not doing" might have brought up (if only slight) a bit of angst for you.

This is not the same as doing nothing. Allow me to explain what I have come to settle into as "not doing". Admittedly, most of my early parenting days consisted of continual doing and reacting to something in this moment with a temporary fix. I was on continual high alert and ready to go to battle, as necessary.

It often felt as though a lump of stress stayed poised for unleashing just beneath the surface and would bubble up and over. What I was doing began to overtake who I was trying to BE. The calm, peaceful Zen-like master, who had been one with the Universe during meditation mere hours before was barking out orders in a shrill-voice and usually over socks on the floor or dishes left in the sink!

"Not doing" is the birthing place for doing. It is the stance we assume, the breath we take in, and the awareness we step into that allows for clear, right action. It looks like pausing when you observe the socks (for the 100th time) all over the floor, before responding. It allows for clear, concise direction.

Not that moments do not arise that require "high alert". I have had to leap a few chairs to unleash a choke-able from a toddler's hand before ingestion. But, we hit the pause button for a moment so that when we do "act" it is from the place inside ourselves that already knows what needs to be done and allows us to do it without all of the veins popping out of our necks!

4

The Tao is empty and deep; when used it is never used up.

I don't know about you, but often as a parent, I have felt "used up". There are moments, days and even weeks when there seems to be more "to do's" than I have the time or energy for. Walking through autism with my son, with therapies, most of which I did myself, was rigorous. There were days I fell into bed fully clothed wondering if I could do this one more day. Growing into a greater awareness of connectedness and "being", I recognized how a lot of my efforts were focused on doing things, but also on trying to maintain some sort of control and balance in my life. It seemed I was spending a lot of energy struggling with and against my life.

As I started to settle into the concept of living the Tao, I recognized that when I am centered and breathing deeply into my Divine Self and Connectedness, there was an endless well that was "never used up". What it looked like was stopping. I stopped fighting with messy rooms (although a "pick up the floor, so I can vacuum up life forms off the floor once a week" was still a good idea), furniture that showed "kid ware", unmade beds (gasp!), kids who wouldn't eat their broccoli (despite all my best efforts to make it attractive!), and letting go of my agenda for what wanted to happen. As I would breathe into each moment as it arose, I realized there was always enough – for that moment. However, if I was caught in my head about what HAD happened, or what would happen in the future, the energy (that was fully available for THIS moment) was scattered and my well would run dry.

Stopping to take a breath and say, "Where am I?" and bringing ourselves back to the present moment connects us to the endless supply in the "well". In this state, we find the reality of "in doing nothing, everything is done." We just have to be willing to let go of everything else. The biggest "everything else" is our own expectations. We let go of expectations of what should be, expectations of ourselves and expectations of our children. If we can let go and let what wants to happen – happen, not only does our "cup runneth over", a great sense of peace and harmony bubbles over as well.

5

The Tao stays in the middle between the "good" and the "bad" giving birth to both... The more it is used, the more there is, the more you speak of it, the less you fully understand. Hold on to the center.

Balance. The Tao speaks of "the middle way", the place in the center that resides between good and bad. As we parent, we strive to find this middle way. As we stay grounded and centered, we stop "taking sides" or even finding the need to call anything good or bad. We hold onto the center, which resides deep within us and is unshakeable.

The beauty of the Tao is that the more we "tap into it" – the more that it becomes available to us. How do we do this? We start by sitting each moment, before the day erupts, in a few moments of quiet to find the center of our Being. This is the place from which all else flows. As we connect to this each day, we can remind ourselves in the middle of chaos of "the order" we have within, simply by dropping into our breath and connecting to the ever-present, ever-flowing Tao energy. It is so easy to get caught up in everyday activities and the whirl of the day consumes us and we are vacillating from one extreme to the other. Our children bump around, getting to know themselves, their limits and how life pushes back. They go from one end (we might label this "bad" if we did not step back and see it for what it is) to the other (perhaps calling it "good" as it fits in with our expectations). Yet, in the center, we see that both are necessary for our child to find out who they are, where the boundaries lie and how to find their own balance. "The more we talk, the less we understand." So, as we quiet our mind, we can listen, both with our ears and eyes but mostly with the calm centered "being-ness" of who we are to what our child is actually saying and doing.

Behavior is a language and when we are centered we begin looking for clues as to what our child is saying and communicating. We talk less, and understand more. We stop labeling and begin to look to really see, "What is my child trying to tell me or show me with this behavior?" In this we find our center and connect more deeply with our child.

When we connect and open our heart chakra, we can look clearly to the intention of our child's behavior. What need were they trying to have met? What were they trying to accomplish? When we are able to connect with this, their "missed" behavior makes more sense and we are able to redirect them toward a behavior that hits their mark. Everyone wins. The child gets their need/s met, and we get to have behavior that is more in alignment with what we find acceptable.

6

The Tao is The Great Mother: empty yet you cannot use it up; inexhaustible, it supports endless possibilities. It is always within you. You can use it any way you want.

I love the reference of the Tao, the life force within us as The Great Mother. Mother is the nurturer, giver, unconditionally loving presence that "feeds" and bathes us in Her warmth. When truly connected to this Presence, we are "empty" (as in nothing impedes the flow of the Divine) yet, inexhaustible, which is different than not ever being tired! There is an ever-present level of energy that flows through us - doing the doing.

The "trick" in life, and in parenting is 1) finding this Presence and 2) staying connected to it. In parenting, what this has looked like for me, is suspending the whirling thoughts (what groceries do I need to get, what bills need to be paid, oh, and where is the permission slip I need to sign and get back for my child's field trip...on and on...) while being in the presence of my child/children. When I see my daughter, do I light up and does SHE see this? Or does it look and sound like, "You need to get ready for school, brush your teeth, did you do your homework, where's your backpack?...on and on..." It is so easy to get caught up in trying to make them better people, that we forget that they are already inherently perfect. The Tao seeks to flow through us to our children, but we can often impede it with the "doing".

Imagine you meet your best friend for coffee. Time is precious, so this is merely a once a month date. When you see her for the first time in a month, you begin to tell her ways of improving herself, or comment on all of the things that are "wrong" with her. No, our impulse is to run up, hug her and tell her how wonderful it is to see her, ash her how she is doing and find out what is going on in her life.

What would it look (and feel) like if each time we saw our child (be it first thing in the morning, right after school, etc.) that we "lit" up and our child saw that we "really saw" them and that more than anything we were just happy to BE with them? If our "mirror" reflecting back to them showed them how beautiful, wonderful and completely adored they were...I wonder what that would do to *their* being-ness.

Seems like all the "doing" stuff would pale in comparison to that!

7

The Master is always behind the scenes and that is why she is "ahead". She remains one with all things, because she is non-attached. She has released the part of her that is "not real" and remembers her Oneness with all things. Thus, she is always full.

The Master stays "behind." She stays in the calm, serene space behind the curtain, behind all that is happening, observing, and finding clarity and her center. She gets "ahead", not by racing herself into oblivion, but by staying behind what is happening and allowing what is happening to play out in front of her without being attached to it. "She is detached from all things". She is not invested in an outcome – only what is happening in the moment and her contribution to it. Is she adding to the problem or taking away from it?

In the middle of a melt-down, staying behind looks like dropping to your knees, breathing deeply, slowly and connecting with the "reptilian" brain-state your child is in. This is a brain-state that is very rudimentary and will not respond well to talking. As you ensure their safety, you are not attached to what happens (who is looking at you making judgments, whether or not the child can be "talked out" of their feelings in the moment), you are merely present, calm, serene, and "behind" it all. Sometimes talking softly, sometimes you are just "being" with the child, allowing them to have their feelings. Perhaps you hold them, if that is helpful, perhaps you stay lovingly "unattached" (which is different than detaching – which feels like withdrawing love).

When the storm passes, in that same unflustered presence, the child is welcomed home to their state of balance with warm, loving arms and you become "one with them" because you never got caught in the cross-winds of the storm – you remained in the "I" of the storm. Too often, we are so focused on a result that we forget to be fully present in the process of what is happening. What is happening is where the lesson is and where the blessing is, if we are willing to "stay behind", be unattached, let go of our lower selves, we truly will be always and forever perfectly fulfilled.

It begins with the connection to our Higher Source and continues when we maintain that connection – even in the middle of a storm!

8

The Tao is like water, which washes over everything, nourishing and releasing. Think simply, be fair, and giving, without controlling. Do what you love and live completely in the "now". When you love the essence of who you are without comparison or competition, you gain the respect of everyone.

In parenting, our supreme good arises from the stillness within and flows through us like water, nourishing all things without trying at all. It is because we are in alignment with our True Selves, so our being-ness is whole and complete. Our mere presence provides a place of comfort, safety and love. Our thoughts are simple in that we stay out of our heads. We recognize the thoughts that arise, but we operate from our heart-space; we allow love to do the thinking and dictating of action in our lives.

There is no need to control, because we see the divine perfection in all beings and things – even when it appears as if all is in total chaos. We trust the process of reorganization (much like that of clearing out a cluttered closet – a lot of stuff has to come out, some of it tossed in the process before we can put things back in – in an orderly fashion). We recognize our attempts to control our children, their behavior and who they "be" comes from a deep level of fear. Releasing this fear allows us to "flow like water" in love.

We become completely present, aware of what is going on with no judgments of comparison on how we are doing because our focus has shifted from "doing" to being. We are watching, observing, and loving from a place that sees beyond our sensory perception. We "see" with x-ray vision of love.

What does this "look" like? It looks like seeing the child behind the messy room. In finding their loveable-ness, we find our own. We reconcile with our own selves our own worthiness just because we are alive and we are able to give this away to our children. We can still expect them to clean their rooms, and offer to help them if they are overwhelmed, but the underlying message is always one of complete and total unconditional love. The message is what you do is less important that who you are. When we teach wholeness (by modeling it ourselves) what our children learn is that right action flows from right alignment with the truth of who we all are – Divine Beings- whole and perfect!

I do not imagine that water worries where it will go. It isn't in the flow; it IS the flow. Learning this simple act of surrender in parenting allows us to flow with life. Life is going to "take us" there anyway. The question is, what state would we prefer to arrive there in – one of frustration, anxiety and fear, or one of complete peace, joy and love?

9

Hold your cup under water and it will eventually spill over. If you sharpen your knife too much, it will become dull. If you run after money, you will never obtain enough. When you care what other's think, you become a prisoner to them. Do your work, then let it go – this is the Tao – the path to peace.

Often, we try to cram a lot into a day, and into the lives of our children. Most of this stems from a desire to enrich their lives with experiences and opportunities, perhaps ones we ourselves never had. But it can be too much and things start to spill over. How much is enough? How much time do we spend (and teach our children to do the same) chasing after things? Do we end up having meals in the car between shuffling from soccer, to gymnastics, to piano lessons to more of the same for our other children? Are we measuring ourselves against others and caring what they might think or if we are doing enough for our children?

Over the years, having had 5 children in my house, I have found that life gets lived in the simple moments. What children remember are not the lessons and organized activities.

Although some have a passion for a particular thing and run with it, in general, all of these "filling of the bowl" activities we put into our children tend to just spill out.

The simple, yet memorable moments arise when there is time to just be. when a silly song gets sung, spontaneously or a game gets played or fun erupts – for no reason at all. Our children are not asking for more "to do" when they say they are bored. They want a connection and stimulation – something that speaks to their being-ness. When we continuously give our children something to do, they have very little time to wiggle around with becoming. Becoming comes from no-thing. There has to be a place for it to be birthed and that doesn't happen in the midst of a flurry of activities.

When we "do our work" and then are able to step back from it because there is very little doing. We do what makes sense and arises in the moment but from a conscious place. In stopping for just a moment to evaluate what we are doing we can begin to decipher how much of it is just our avoidance with being fully present, in the absence of distraction with our children.

10

Can you truly love people without having an agenda? Can you allow life to take its course in even the most important things? Can you be like a little baby and not cling to anything? Can you nurture and hold without possessing, can you do without clinging to results, can you lead without controlling? This is the Tao. Allowing.

Parenting is a course in letting go. In the beginning, our children come to us ("we have them but do not possess them") helpless, and we need to care for their every need or they will not survive. As they grow into independence we relinquish this control, little by little so that they are able to live their own lives. It becomes difficult at times to lead them without imposing our will. We get very good at making sure they are o.k. and when they begin to make decisions that are outside our definition of "o.k.", it gets scary. Letting the most vital matters evolve and simply take their course becomes a scary and risky proposition for us. This doesn't mean that we do not intervene when necessary or guide and provide healthy boundaries. It just means we stop imposing our will all of the time, lead by example and recognize as our children grow and change, that they are going to have to make decisions that won't always seem to work out. But they do. As they are all lessons designed to grow our souls.

As we give birth and nourish, hold on without holding back and give love, understanding and compassion without expectations, we relinquish control. Not because we couldn't figure this all out for our children and ensure that they "get it right". It is because we *have* figured it out that we relinquish control recognizing this is our child's time to learn. We simply step back from our own minds and understand all things – all things are well, Divinely designed and from a centered place "act" without doing, as the right and perfect answer always comes forth.

This often just looks like waiting a few extra moments for them to figure it out or waiting for their response. When we slow down and recognize that our child is in the process of learning, we begin to allow more time for this to take place.

11

The spokes of a wheel join together and there in the center is emptiness. This is what allows it to move. We can mix clay together to make a pot, but it is the emptiness inside that allows us to "hold" something in it. You can make doors and windows and create a house, but the inner space is what allows us to live within it. We work with the form, but it is the formless that we truly use.

The essence of "The Tao of Parenting" is *being* the center that makes the wagon move. So often we are fragmented and identify more with the spokes – going in all directions. When we are truly centered, the wagon moves effortlessly. In a society so enamored with stuff and results and end product, we often neglect the intangible, the *emptiness* that "holds whatever we want". In parenting, we can be so busy filling up – our days, our calendars, our homes, and our children that we neglect the actual space we create from. Do we stop and teach our children to stop? When we are hurried, do we take a moment to stop, take a breath, re-center and move from the center and not try to move from the spoke?

"It is the inner space that makes it livable." How much time are we dedicating to tend to the "inner space" of ourselves and our children? Parenting is all about cultivating a life. It is about modeling and teaching skills that our children will utilize the rest of their lives. It is easy to get distracted by the things we are *doing* (soccer, gymnastics, homework, playdates, drama class, cheer, baseball, and the list goes on and on). We actually think we are preparing them for life when we provide them opportunities in abundance to do things. It is not that these things are inherently "bad" – it's just they can often masquerade as "who" we really are when in fact they are just things that we do.

When we hit the pause button we evaluate what actual skills for the *rest of our child's lives*, are they acquiring? What happens when things get hard (and they will) and stress piles on (and it does) and life gets messy? Have we taught and modeled coping mechanisms, centering and a connection to the "truth" of who our children really are?

Do we remind them they are not their grades, their trophies or anything that they do? The essence of who they are lies in the center, in the emptiness – the awareness or witness to all of these things – but not the things themselves. We want to fill our children up with the things that will sustain them when they don't win, when they cannot have it all, when they don't always succeed. When we teach them about who they really are, then, what comes and goes, when life challenges them, they are in the center and not pulled into the whirlwind. They recognize their non-being as WHO they are. Then whatever comes before them, they are standing in their truth and nothing can shake them.

12

All the colors blind and all the sounds deafen and all flavors will numb the taste. Thoughts cloud the mind. Desires weaken the heart. The Master looks at the world but trusts what she "knows" and allows things to come and go. She keeps her heart wide open.

Our senses not only lie to us, but they can bombard us with so much information that we get lost in them. We want so much for our kids. Our desires for them, although coming from a good place, can wither - not only our hearts, but theirs as well. What about what *they* want? I'm not just talking about wanting to eat candy all day, stay up late, and not go to school. I'm talking about the desires buried deep within their souls that are calling to them. Maybe dancing is not their thing. Maybe my son is just not into sports. Can we be OK with what wants to happen? Can we observe the world, but look deep within to what "feels" right, even when it might go against the grain?

Allowing things (and people) to come and go in our lives gets tricky. We don't mind letting things go when we don't want them. It's hard to let things go that we actually wanted to stay: relationships, jobs, homes, even our children growing up and moving away. It is easy to accept things as they are, when we are content with what that is. However, life being a conduit for continual growth, it doesn't always work that way. Sometimes we are pushed into growing in areas of our lives we weren't particularly interested in growing in.

If we only view the world by what we see, hear or taste and especially what we think, we will continually be drawn into the drama of what is playing out on the stages of our lives. If we can step back behind the curtain and peer into the innate wisdom of our inner selves, we may catch a glimpse of true peace and our hearts may just burst open and then the sky truly is the limit...both for us and our children. We just need to take those moments to withdraw from our external senses to see within and to teach our children to do the same.

13

To be successful or to fail is equally dangerous. Having either makes one fearful. If you are going up a ladder or going down, you are shaky. When you are standing on the ground, you maintain your balance. Trust in the way things are.

It seems in life, and parenting is no exception, we are always racing towards some "finish" line or some pre-determined expectation of what success looks like. We feel there is a "right" way to do things and a wrong way. When pursuing some position in parenting, whether going up or down, our position remains shaky. Finding balance is about finding our center, on the ground, not longing for something "out there".

What does this look like? It looks like loving what is in front of us. Maybe that is a messy house, because we have chosen to play Barbies or Hot Wheel cars instead of picking up and doing laundry. It looks like taking a less-paying job, a smaller house or an older car so that our expenses aren't overwhelming us and we have to work two jobs to cover the expenses instead of spending time with our children. It means stepping back from the continual review of what needs to be fixed in us and our children or changed and loving how we show up and embracing the imperfection within our own Divine Selves. It is sitting down in the middle of the mess and being at peace with it. It is knowing NOW that it truly is perfect and it won't take many years from now when we look back, for us to understand that the "things" in life that are important were never things at all.

They were moments of pure bliss that erupted when a spontaneous fort was created, s'mores were made and indulged in, we went to the park with the kids and laid on the grass and looked at clouds, we made home-made pretzels and watched a movie all cuddled-up together. These moments can happen. When we love the world as ourselves – and our children and families are our world, we care for them, not in a way that merely tends to their basic needs (brush your teeth, comb your hair, do your homework), but cares for the sweet little ways they want a piece of us—really us – the "fun" us that drops the "parental controls" and switches channels where we can just "be" with them and play with them.

As we stand on solid ground, dropping to our knees on occasion to stare into the eyes of our wonder child, what do we see?   More importantly, what do THEY see?   Do they see someone who *sees* them?

Are you someone your child wants to play with?

14

Look at it and it can't be seen. It is colorless. Listen and it can't be heard. It is noiseless. Reach and it can't be grasped. It is formless. It cannot be named. It returns back into the formless. Follow it and it cannot be found.

Have you ever noticed it is very difficult to quantify your love for your child? There are no words that can adequately express how you feel. There are words to express how you demonstrate your love for your child – but the essence, the love cannot be seen with the eye, nor heard with the ear or grasped in any way. It just is. This is the formlessness of the Tao that we are talking about. It is a way of being that has no words. It comes from the deep wisdom that we all innately come from. As we tap into our essence and we are able to connect with this same essence in our child, everything changes.

The to-do's narrow down to what is necessary, and that which builds a greater sense of connection and love. All the extraneous distractions fall away as we recognize that what our children really need is our presence. They need a place where love resonates from the deepest place, our essence, and has no conditions. Imagine sitting in a room where no matter how you showed up, all there was to greet you was love. It didn't need to "fix" you, move you any faster, be disappointed in your choices, tell you what to do and how to do it, not disapprove of your clothes, friends, grades, condition of your room, lack of manners.... It was merely a space where every cell in your body was saturated with unconditional love.

Who couldn't become anything they ever wanted to be in that space?

This is where "doing without doing" makes sense. When there is a foundation that emanates pure love and acceptance, whatever needs to be done is effortless effort. True connection takes effort to drop out of our heads, which contains lists of things to do, flaws that need to be altered, expectations that need to be met, and into our heart which is pure, ever-flowing love that just wants to wash over our child and love them up. It's not that things don't get done. They do. That is just not ever the focus.

What this looks like is taking a few moments each day, or a Saturday morning and just "being" with your child. There are no errands at this moment, and no need to have our child do anything. Curl up with a great story in your jammies, or color pictures together. Go to the park and really play with your child instead of reading a book on the bench. Have a spontaneous picnic. Find a moment each day where you connect with the essence of your child with no expectations – breathe deep into your heart, remembering all the sweet little wonders of your child and allow that love to flow in and all around them. You will be amazed at how it changes them. You will be amazed at how it changes you.

15

The ancient Masters wandered through the mystery and could not discern it, therefore they described its appearance. Those following the Tao were cautious and aware. They were considerate like a guest, fluid like ice melting under the sun. They were malleable, like a block of wood. They were open and clear. Do you have the patience to wait until the muddy water goes back to the bottom and the water is clear? Can you wait until the right thing to do becomes clear and obvious? The Master seeks after nothing. She has no expectations and is fully present, therefore is open to all things.

Imagine as a parent being so present. To be careful, alert, courteous, fluid, shapeable, receptive and clear. Wow! To be able to go with what is happening and being open to it is a skill in life that would serve in so many areas – not just parenting. But, in particular, in parenting it can be the difference between sanity and well, just crazy!

Having the patience to just sit, waiting for the mud to settle is one that does not come natural to our ever-controlling brains. I don't know about your house, but in my house there is quite a bit of "mud" on a daily basis. The boundless energy of children is continually moving and it can stir things up a bit. Although we do not want to bridle this beautiful flowing energy, we might want to direct it, teaching them to regulate it and allow for some "settling" time.

We can allow/create this for ourselves as well. Allowing energy to flow in, through and as us while allowing is not always a practice we invoke in. When we let the mud settle (as in allow things to just "be" and not muddle in them...couldn't resist the use of the world "muddle" ☺), we can find a solution to anything...we become clear and the problem or rather the solution to the problem becomes clear.

We do this by starting each day settled. We find a moment to breathe, set the intention for a love-filled, peaceful day and reconnecting to this peaceful place as often as necessary throughout the day. Once we know what it feels like, we can visit there often. As we are parenting on purpose, our children can catch us being clear.

16

Relinquish the thoughts in your mind and still your heart. Empty your mind of all thoughts. Let your heart be at peace. Everything flourishes and returns to its roots. We call this tranquility – returning to one's nature. When we do this, we become clear. Then the self fears no danger.

Thoughts run rampant for us all. There seems to be no end to the litany of things that run the gamut in our wild, open minds. It is difficult to empty, as it seems there is a constant influx of thoughts that are continually refilling our minds. I have found that stepping back and watching the turmoil tends to be a better way than trying to empty every thought from my mind. As I see it arise, I become *aware* that I am aware and from that place I get to choose what to do with it. Whether I believe the thought that something shouldn't be happening, or that I need to go clean the kitchen instead of spending time with my child, and on and on is mine to decide. Awareness just puts a little space around the thought so that I get to view it as something I have a decision about, rather than a constant barrage of orders I am being given from the non-stop chatter in my mind.

When I realize that where I come from is an eternal space of grace, a never-ending, continuously flowing stream of energy I can rest, I can be nonplussed by what shows up. As I know that I already have what I need...be that time, energy, money or the answer to a seemingly unsolvable problem.

The only difficulty is in the "When I realize" part of this sentence...what does it take to realize?

Time. Quiet time and space to connect with the Divinity within me and a gentle reminder that although my inclination is to save the world and all its inhabitants, I merely need save myself. The rest will flow easily and readily from me. If I only take the *time* to realize. I see with my "eyes" what is real. Everything else, all the stories that keep me from my peace are mere illusions.

When I see clearly, there truly is nothing to fear.

17

With the highest of rulers, people do not know they even have them. Next, people love and praise them. The next level, people fear them, and finally, at the lowest level, people despise them and do not trust them. The Master speaks very little and just "does" and when it is done, they all say, "Wow...we did it all by ourselves!"

Conscious parenting looks effortless. When one parents from this place, the answers arise by themselves, clear, precise. Our children love us, not fear us. As we continually find the place of surrender, serenity and clarity, there is less talking and more acting. When we are done, the child feels as though they have solved the problem themselves (whether this is choosing what to wear, what activity to engage in, what class to take, who to date, what occupation to choose, etc.). We parent in such a way that it facilitates right action from our child.

Sounds blissful, doesn't it? What does it look like, you ask? It looks like being content with not knowing all of the answers and trusting life's ambiguity, and risking judgment from other parents when you allow your child to make decisions and live with the consequences. It looks like holding back your opinion so your child can figure things out for themselves and not saying "I told you so" if they don't.

There is a precarious balance that if we begin it early, our children get to learn to "master" themselves. Unfortunately, we tend to be light on boundaries at the beginning of parenting and try to tighten the reins when our unbridled children hit adolescence. This results in a whole lot of resistance and "bit biting!" If we taught self-discipline when a child is open to receive it, it would go more smoothly. A child learns the word, "no" by first, us being the No (when they are infants we choose for them what is good for them and what must be said "no" to). Then, we transition to telling them "No" (no fingers in light sockets, no running in the streets). Lastly, they tell us "No" (oh, they do this so well!) Often, we are afraid of the middle stage. When we can tell our children "No" with love and show them a better way it goes a long way to teaching them where the guard-rails are for their living.

Then, as they grow, these well-established guidelines become the space in which they wiggle around as teenagers.

18

When the great Tao is forgotten, benevolence and justice rule and intelligence comes forth. When there is no peace in the family, filial piety begins.

Who doesn't want to have peace in their family? Filial piety is a sense of duty to one's family. When there is no peace, we become an obligation to one another. That sure doesn't feel good. How do we go from blissful, sweetness with our newborn, to "duty", which is so heavy and filled with unmet expectations? Peace within our family begins with a commitment to living consciously, "in the now" and accepting of what is. We respond to one another with a sense of respect, regard for individuality and reverence for the Divine Light within each one.

What tends to happen is that we get distracted by the *personality* that is housing this light. Sometimes it can look like a dim bulb to us. How do we brighten this light in our children? How do we even see it?

We begin with a connection to it. We do this by dropping expectations of how they *should* show up and accepting how they *are* showing up. If the behaviors they are displaying are "missing" the mark of what is acceptable, we look to the intention of the behavior...what are they trying to accomplish? What inherent need (which they have an absolute right to have met) is my child trying to meet – albeit in a "missing the mark" kind of way? When we connect to the intention, then we can soften our hearts, open up to our child in a way that allows us to "teach" (the original term parent, comes from the Latin word "parenth" which is to teach), our child a way of getting their need met using a behavior that is acceptable.

If their behavior lies within an acceptable range, yet we are having a hard time accepting it, we are open to evaluating this and making adjustments in our expectations as well. When we remain in an open-heart space, we find there is a lot of wiggle room for changes. If our goal is to create peace, we will be lead into ways in which we can obtain this. We must be willing to *do* something different if we want different results.

19

End wisdom and get rid of knowledge and people are happier. Get rid of benevolence and abandon righteousness and people return to piety and charity. End cunning and discard profit. These things are superficial and insufficient. Show plainness and simplicity, reduce selfishness and decrease desires and allow all things to take their course.

Throw away wisdom and knowledge? That doesn't even make sense. But, if we look closer, what is "wisdom and knowledge"? They are *someone else's* experience and eclectic ideas of how things should look and our belief about how something should be. If we allow each individual to find their own way, experience their life and make conclusions based on that experience, would they not be happier?

Have you ever had a movie review from a friend that after you saw the movie did not match yours at all? If you had the movie review before you went to see the movie, did it color your experience?

When we have an idea about how someone should experience life, especially our children, we tend to hand them answers before they ask questions or if they question our answers, we might even be disturbed by this. Industry and profit (looks like good or bad) in our house – when we throw this concept out, we don't have children who have to take sides. There are varying degrees of what works and what does not work. We can look at behavior as on the spectrum of either moving towards hitting the behavior that meets their need (and we find acceptable), to the other end of the spectrum where the child is "missing" (as in Missed-behavior) the mark, and the behavior is unacceptable to us and varying degrees therein.

When we stay in the center (balanced and conscious) we are able to see things from all angles and see how we can help our child move along the spectrum of behaviors to have their needs met, AND have the behavior be acceptable to us.

20

Stop thinking, and end your problems. What difference between yes and no? What difference between success and failure? Must you value what others value, avoid what others avoid? How ridiculous! Other people are excited, as though they were at a parade. I alone don't care, I alone am expressionless, like an infant before it can smile, I am different from ordinary people. I drink from the Great Mother's breasts.

Stop thinking. It sounds like a ridiculously and hopelessly trite solution. How in the world can one *stop* thinking? Quite frankly, I don't know if it is possible to STOP. However, I do know I have personally hit the pause button on occasion. It is from the "freeze frame" experience that a true, clear and helpful picture to whatever was going on at the time was "framed". How do we do this? With the endless drone of things to do and children to attend to, in the midst of a parenting moment, how do we hit pause? The first way we do this is become aware that we are continually commentating on what is going on in the first place. There is a chatter happening that is dictating how we experience what is going on and then subsequently, how we deal with it. Next, we stop and breathe.

For instance, as we look at our child's mess that they have recently made, how many of us have chatter something like this, "I cannot believe these towels on the floor. I have asked this child 10 times to pick this up and there is food all over the floor, and what is THAT?! Does this child think I am the maid?" And on-and-on the "chatter" goes. When we step back, ask the question, "Who is having this thought?" We get to hit the pause button on thinking. Only then can we see that there is no real "yes or no" (right or wrong), there is simply our interpretation of what is happening, based on our past experience. We have the ability, if we choose to look at the situation differently. We then get to *respond* to the situation with clarity, precision and most importantly love. If we approach the situation, as in the example above, from love, it doesn't mean that we tolerate messy living situations. However, we do not attach to the "why" our child left the room like this (as in, they think we're the maid and have no consideration for us at all). We take the "blame" out of it, see what is there, state the facts, in love and with boundaries. "These towels need to be picked up, the food put away and that fungi over there thrown away."

We choose what we value by what we do and say. Many people are incongruent about what they "say" they value and what they actually "do". For example, I love and value my children and want them to grow up knowing & feeling this but my actions may value a clean house or good grades instead. When we step back, we get to look at what do we really value (picture-perfect clean rooms, or happy, creative unconditionally loved children? Bustling, "make-it-out-of-nothing" activities in the backyard, or back-to-back, structured activities after school)? When we choose on purpose what we want for our child and their experience, we get to look at – *really* look at what we truly value.

When we drop into "expressionless" – this is not spiritual Botox! ☺ This is a matter of being so centered, so calm, so rational...that nothing moves us –one way or the other. When we stop and breathe deeply, it connects us to this place. The kids bring us flowers, it is a good day, the kids bring us F's on their report cards, and it is a good day. This center, this life flowing through us, steps beyond what is happening, to get under it and see what really matters. We become different in our parenting, because our endless nourishment comes from the Divine – that is in and all around and we truly want for nothing. Which means we do not "want" for flowers our children bring us, for we have our own blossom within that adds fragrance to our lives...our "feel goods" do not come from them, they are just bonuses! And when they have F's on *their* report cards...they belong to *them* – not us. We have done our own educational experience, and this is theirs. We love them, support them and offer resources for them to have a more successful educational experience, if they choose. But, we do not own their experience. We have our own Source of filling up. We love them unconditionally, and point them to their Source as well.

21

The appearance of great virtue follows the Tao. She can be at one with it, even though it is unclear, indistinct there is an image so indistinct and so unclear that she lets go of all "ideas" and clings to nothing. She allows all things.

What is "The Tao" anyway? It is difficult to put into words as it is a word to describe "the way" or "the path" or "life". How can you sum *that* up? How can you sum up that which supports "the way" or is all there is and not on "the path" or supports "life"? It is very difficult – yea, even ungraspable. But, we find a way to settle into it by not clinging to anything. It is the pause button. It is the space, the little tiny space in between breaths where we are neither breathing, nor not breathing – we are suspended. When we learn to start living in the suspended moments, our parenting (breathing in and out) becomes effortless.

What does this look like? It looks like parenting on purpose, consciously. It looks like identifying what works and what doesn't work with your parenting style and moving towards better ways of resolving conflict. It looks like asking one's self, "What qualities do I want my child to have?" or, "Who do I want my child to be when they leave my care?" When we ask this question, we parent "backwards" by looking at what it takes to create this "mensch" or whole person. Hint: it doesn't look like bribing, yelling or giving into demands.

A person who is responsible, needs to be given responsibility at every age. A two-year old can choose between shirts and understand the consequence of having to come inside when they run in the street. We teach perspective taking and kindness. A two year old can understand words like, "Ouch" if they hit you and know that they have created pain. A five year old can be asked when observing another child suffering, "What do you think they are feeling?" A twelve-year-old can be taken to the mall to observe similarities of all people and how we are all connected. Creating a child who is responsible, caring and trustworthy starts when they are younger.

We often teach our children to lie unknowingly by not accepting their true feelings ("I don't want to hug Grandma, because she smells funny." To which we respond, "No she doesn't, you are going to hurt her feelings. Go hug her.") We can respond with loving understanding, "Hmmm...I see your dilemma. Can you think of a solution?" They will usually respond with holding their breath or something. But, at least we have allowed "the truth" of their feelings and helped them navigate and come up with a solution, without shame.

As a challenge, regardless of your child's age, look at what qualities you hope your child will leave your home with. Then, ask yourself, "Do I display these qualities?" If not, there's your work. If so, then look at ways in which you can facilitate the organic assimilation of these traits.

22

Yield and remain whole. Be low and you are filled. Be worn out and you become renewed; have a little and receive much. By not contending, the world cannot contend with them. If you want to be given it all, let it all go.

Often in approaching parenting, we present as if we are the "experts" when in truth, often, we struggle in many of the same ways our children do. The fears might look different in us, but they still might be dictating some of our choices or debilitating us in some way. There is an assumption that because one is capable of having children, one has all of the necessary tools to lead this precious being into wholeness. Sometimes we wonder what "wholeness" looks like for ourselves.

How do we become whole? First, we admit that we are not the experts, and we allow ourselves to be "partial". D.W. Winnicott, a child expert, calls this the "good enough parent". I like to call it, "The I am enough parent". In that space, in that "partial" space, we not only recognize that we are not "experts", we embrace that we are mere humble students at the feet of the "masters" who will help us to straighten out our "crooked" selves. But, first we must allow ourselves to be partial, crooked, empty and "die" to some truths and long-held beliefs about ourselves.

In raising our children, we have a chance to be "given everything" and to be made whole and in the process facilitate wholeness for these precious beings who have come into our care. But, first, we must give everything up – we must give up the belief that we are not enough, that we must do everything perfect or that our children must somehow redeem us for all of the "wrongs" we have done along the way. When we give up expectations, beliefs that do not serve us, and demands that our children somehow fit into an agenda of our making, we open up to the possibility of "everything".

As we look at our children, we see them as whole and perfect and in need of our own wholeness so that we come from a centered place of "enough" and we allow them the freedom to make their own choices, live with those consequences, and grow from the experiences. This doesn't always look "pretty" and we often have to die just a little to the "idea" of what parenting looks like.

A "good" parent has children who color inside the lines, get straight A's, make the all-star team, has lots of friends, personality, obeys the rules and essentially makes us look "good" (hence, the "good" parent). A "bad" parent has children who question everything, gets messy sometimes, wiggles around with who they are, tries but might not always get the grades they are capable of because they are often confused as to whether the grades are really "theirs" or ours. Oooh...it looks bad and we often are judged, but never more harshly than we judge ourselves. We navigate these waters and try to apply more pressure to an already broken system.

However, if we can step back and release ("die a little") our expectations of perfection and allow our child to own the "problem" (grades, friends, their experiences) while setting limits and boundaries (a place to do homework, tutors if necessary, appropriate electronic monitoring – shut-down by 9:30 p.m., for example,) we can allow our children to begin to experience life and it's occasional smack-downs in a loving, safe environment and when the consequences are not as great.

Having a child who loves who they are and truly believes they can do anything they want, who is kind and happy. THAT'S everything...and worth giving up anything else!

23

Say what you must, then stop talking. Even the wind does not last all morning and sudden rain does not last all day. When you are open to loss, loss is with you, when you are open to the Tao, the Tao is with you. Open yourself to the Tao and allow everything to go as it will.

How many times as parents do we say the same thing over and over again? What would it look like if we expressed ourselves completely and then stopped talking? Say it once, mean it, and then act. We become like annoying fly-swatters and our children, quite frankly just stop listening. To parent consciously, we want to be like the wind. How clear is it to just point out what we want..."I need those dishes in the sink." Which often looks like, "Every time I come home, there are dishes everywhere, I have asked you to put the dishes in the sink, I'm tired....blah blah blah.."

How many of us learned to do something the first time? Or even the second? If you want to incorporate something into your life, it takes time, discipline, practice and motivation. Our brain integrates information based on frequency, intensity, duration and consistency. A study was conducted with children, and they discovered that the foundation of intelligence is formed, by parents who help children make sense of their world. They do not teach directly, but mediate the experience for the child; poor learners are passive in their experience.

Our children are clever about the things they don't want to do. If they can get out of something even 1 time out of 10, if they're smart, they will! If we can accept this (be at one with "loss"), then we can have peace – we live in the Tao of Now. We say it. We mean it. We back it up with action. Yet, we understand that for children, learning is a continual process and we might have to facilitate the "learning" over and over and in different ways until they really know and understand it. However, we must understand that they will not learn unless they are actively engaged in the process.

Our natural response – our essential, "whole" self – the part that is still connected to our Source, is love. Love moves like wind – blowing away all that no longer matters. In the scheme of life, in the teaching moments, can we be at peace with our roles as teachers and move in love?

24

When you are on your tiptoes, you cannot stand. When you straddle, you cannot walk. When you flaunt yourself, you are not clear, nor distinguished. When you try to define yourself, you cannot know who you really are. When you have power over others, you cannot empower yourself. Do not hold onto your work, just do your job and let it all go.

There's a whole lot of reaching when it comes to parenting. We are constantly being stretched, having to be "ahead" of the learning curve. But, this isn't really serving us. We spend so much time trying to learn and be prepared for what is ahead, we don't remain in the teachable moment of the present. As we define ourselves as parents, we get locked into certain beliefs (about ourselves and our children) that end up dimming everyone's light. To parent consciously, we want to be able to look at ourselves objectively and with some clarity. We also want to relinquish the power (which really looks like control) over others. How do we do this while still guiding our children into adulthood?

Relinquishing control is something none of us do very well. We "cling" to our work as parents because we do not know how to do it differently. Letting go is not giving up or boundary-less parenting. This is not what I am talking about. This is not an unruly household where everyone does what they want. I am speaking to the intention behind how we parent. We ask ourselves, "Who should be handling this right now – me or my child?" We look at situations with eyes wide open and see how we can facilitate learning (not take over and fix everything). This takes time, patience, clarity and a lot of letting go.

How much easier is it to tell our child everything to do – or worse, do it for them? This works. For a time. But at some time, our children will be moving through adolescence and the time to prepare them for this transition is when they are still assimilating the learning. As we foster a respectful and loving relationship with them (not one laced in control), we allow them to make decisions, live with the consequences of said decisions and love them through it all. We aren't punitive, angry or judgmental, because we have released attachment to the outcome. We do what needs to be done, we set up healthy boundaries, we guide when necessary, but we have a heart wide open because we do not have an agenda about what (or who) our child needs to do or become.

When we are centered in this place, we are in accord with the Tao and true life flows effortlessly through us and penetrates right down to the core of our child. I have never seen a problem that could not be handled with more unconditional love.

25

There was something before Heaven and Earth. It is independent and changeless and is regarded as the Mother of the world and called the Tao. It flows in, through and as all things. It is great and thus the whole world is great.

Have you ever tried to define love? Love is so abstract that words seem to fail when trying to encompass all that it is. We can say what it is not. We can say what it does, but there really aren't words for what love is. Do you remember holding your child for the first time and the overwhelming sense of emotion that you did not even know you could possess that washed over you?

This is a mere taste of the Tao. Nestled in the Tao, we are being lived. When we open up to being lived, it is effortless. As it flows, just like a river through a canyon, it cuts away all that is no longer necessary. This might look like giving up habits thoughts, beliefs, language, and even control. It might mean embracing fears and allowing the energy to flow through and wear away that which is keeping you from your best self and the part of you that is whole and can truly connect with this precious "Being" in your care.

We tend to see our children as inherently "ours" when in fact, they are their own Selves with their own life path, soul growth, and work to do. We are merely tour guides throughout this mission. We get confused about their work and ours. We see things in them that bring up our own work (which is exactly what it is intended to do – so that we might work through it and heal it and move on), yet we often get fixated on changing them to make ourselves more comfortable.

This tends to happen a lot through adolescence. I have met many an adult who were very wounded during this time. It's not a "pretty" time, as we come face-to-face with the "in betweens" and as humans, we do not like this gray area so much. We like black or white, right or wrong, but rarely do we like it in the middle. It brings up fears, confusion, and a general sense that we are "not who we are to be yet", nor are we who we were. This can bring up a lot of places in ourselves that have yet to be healed. To parent consciously, we must be aware of what is "our stuff" and what is our child's. Can we allow the Tao to cut away that which is wounding us so that it can flow freely as our child gets to wiggle around with who they are becoming and live the life they charted? Or do we get caught up in our own details and try to control the outcome?

Just creating some space and awareness around this will allow us to truly be present with our child. And when things do come up, we can soften towards ourselves and parent our own self back to wholeness. We deserve the same ever-present, all-loving (with no conditions) kindness we are giving to our child. As the Tao flows through and touches others, it cannot help but heal us.

If we only allow it to flow.

26

Heaviness is the root of lightness and quietness, the master of restlessness. The Master can travel an entire day without ever leaving her home. She sees all, yet stays tranquil within herself. When she is light, flitting all about, she loses her roots and when she is restless, she loses her mastery.

How comfortable are you in your own skin? Does being alone scare you? Do you feel "at home" with yourself? Can you be at peace without ever leaving the comforts of your own soul? There is a lot of restless parent syndrome these days. So many parents flit about to and from taking their kids from karate, to volleyball, to track, to gymnastics, to play groups to organized sports and the list goes on and on. Very few children today have unorganized play (even play "dates" are more popular than just playing in the backyard). How many kids actually spend time in the backyard daily making something out of nothing? Kids say, "I'm bored" on a regular basis as they are so used to being entertained. Go to any restaurant and see all the "i-babysitters" as kids are so "bored" waiting for food they need an electronic device to pass the time.

We are creating a generation of kids who are restless and cannot stay serenely in themselves because we are not able to show them what this looks like. We've lost touch with our "roots" which keeps us blowing all around with no direction what-so-ever. Our children are looking to us for grounding. There's a song that says, "I've gotta have roots before branches" and never is that more true than with our children. "Roots" looks like staying put and saying "no" to the incessant activities that life threatens to suck us all into. I'm not against involvement, but when is it "too much"? Are we creating an atmosphere of "to and fro" and not enough here and now? We have lost touch with who we are. If we want our children to flourish, to flow and bloom where they are planted, we need to ground them (funny how our term for getting children back on track when they have gone astray is called "grounding").

They need roots. They need to be grounded. But first, we must ground ourselves.

27

A good traveler makes no plans and is not attached to "getting" anywhere. A good artist allows the art to flow through. A good scientist has no fixed ideas and keeps his mind open. The Master is open to all things and can use all situations towards enlightenment. Thus, the good person is the teacher of the bad person and the bad person is the resource for the good person. If we do not understand this, we are confused. This is the great wonder.

As we travel this road of parenting, how many of us have a destination in mind? How content can we be with "no intent upon arriving"? We are so good at lists, goals, objectives, and plans that we have very little room for being led to what wants to happen, with an open mind, being open to all things. It is difficult to see the "good" in what appears to be a "bad" situation.

We are missing the secret to parenting because we are so focused on what we "think" should be happening. We parent the way we were parented (even if we KNOW it didn't work for us) that we miss opportunities for real learning and soul growth – both for ourselves and our children.

We are lost. We have thousands of books on parenting, we take classes, yet, we are still lost because we have lost touch with our True Selves. We aren't available "for all" because we are barely available for ourselves.

Parenting consciously means we are "awake" and aware of what we are doing and why we are doing it. We do not waste opportunities for learning even when they are not convenient. There are so many great opportunities for "real life" in the middle of trying to "arrive" somewhere else. If we are able to stop and breathe into the moment, we can take this "teachable moment" unfolding in living color, right in the middle of the Target store, to teach our child about "no". With compassion, we can stop, get down at eye level, dismiss all the stares that are darting our way, be fully present with patience and simplicity, look into the tearful pleading eyes begging for the candy at the checkout (which is not a bad thing, it is just not appropriate this time and you intuitively know this), and say, "I know. You want candy now. It is dinner time and no candy."

Diane English has a quote I love, "Blessed are the cracked, for they shall let in the light." This amused me, but also loved the wisdom in it. When I was tucking my daughter in one night and she was scared of the dark, she asked me to leave the door

66

open "just a crack, Mommy." I was thinking how very little space we actually need to let light in. When we are willing to open up to new possibilities (in ourselves and in our children), even "just a crack", we might be surprised what seeps in.

28

Know the personal, yet keep to the impersonal: accept the world as it is. If you can accept what is in the world, the Tao will flow within you and you will return to your authentic Self. The world is shaped from nothing like tools from wood. Know the "tools" but understand where they come from. Then you are able to use it all.

Parenting is all about doing what you can, where you are with what you have. Collecting "tools" along the way enables us to utilize greater strategies but ultimately it is not about the "tools" so much as it is about the "wood" – the essence. To accept our parenting world as it is, we can "know" the personal (the details, the minutia) but we want to keep to the "impersonal" which looks like non-attachment. This is different than detachment. Detachment looks like "I don't care." Non-attachment is the highest form of caring. It is love with no conditions. I love you, but do not need you to do anything to earn it – it is offered freely. (Even when you ruin my best pots making mud pies, dent my car or spit "I hate you" in my face).

The "tools" just provide guidelines and a buffer to buy us time to return to our "authentic self" which is the part of us that already knows how to live here. We have just forgotten or over the course of our being parented, have had this part of ourselves wounded. When we operate from our wounded self, we tend to give away what we are, which is wounded...so we wound. It is not intentional, but when we become aware and conscious, we can return to our primal self and the luminous (as in lightened up parts) of our selves get to shed light on the situation, not the dark, scary wounded places.

When my son was younger, he used to cry for his "no one car". We searched everywhere for this mysterious car. We had no idea what he was talking about. Finally, a few days later, he came in, elated and holding the cherished "no one" car. I looked at the side and laughed out loud. There in plain view it said, "No. 1!" Isn't this analogous to how we feel sometimes? We feel (and our children) that we are "no one" when in fact we are No. 1 in God's eyes. We just get lost in the erroneous beliefs, patterns, habits, and thoughts that support the "no one" concept.

We are here to grow our souls. When we feel like "no one" or stumble upon a darkened space, we learn to find the light in the dark. But, we have to be the ones to switch on the light. Our children provide many opportunities for us to do so. This does not look like passive parenting. It is not about allowing our children to run wild. It is about noticing what happened, moving swiftly to action, but always with the non-attachment, unconditional loving space that resides within us.

29

If you want to take the world, control and save it, it cannot be done. The world is sacred and it does not need anyone to improve it. Everything does what it needs to do and in its own time. The Master allows all things without trying to control them – she leaves them alone, keeping to the center.

As mothers, we often want to "save" everything...the skinny, abandoned dog on the street, the environment, our children...we look at everything and everyone as "projects" to be improved. It is our nature to nurture and make things "better" – kiss away boo-boos, improve on recipes, we are even "addicted" to life makeovers. We hire life-coaches and as a society invest in makeovers so much that there are entire shows dedicated to this!

What if it were all perfect just the way it is? Wow. This is hard to take in, when we look around. Yet, the truth is. It is perfect. If we are able to stay in the "center" of it all, we would see this. How can it be perfect, you ask? Because it is. It is the thought that we have to the contrary that creates all the stress in our lives and the expectations we put on our "projects" (mostly our children) that create most of the conflict in our homes and within our own hearts.

Sit with that for a minute.

Our children come through us not to us. We are here to guide them but they do not need to be improved. I don't know about you, but I don't feel so good if I am anyone's "project". No one wants to be "fixed" or improved because that implies that we are inherently broken. If we approach our children as projects (and believe me, they sense that), imagine what that tells them about who they really are?

What would happen to our children if they walked into a room and they felt an unconditional love and acceptance when we saw them? We hugged them and communicated (with more than just words) how loved they were, just because. If we did that and only that, there would be no "saving" necessary.

Of course, this doesn't mean we never tell them to brush their teeth, clean up their rooms or do their homework. But if for a moment every time we "reconnected" they felt only unconditional love and acceptance, they'd fill right on up and spill over and that kind of love IS a sacred world.

30

Whoever uses the Tao in raising children, doesn't try to force thing to happen, forcing their will. When you push, there will be a push back. Violence, even in the form of "well-intentioned" punishment, always backfires upon oneself. The Master does what is hers to do only. She gets that the Universe does not need her to control it and she allows the Tao to flow in her life. She believes in the True Self and does not care what others think.

In working with families over the years, I have noticed that the ones who struggle the most during adolescents are the ones who "controlled" their children growing up. What happens during adolescence is the pushback. We all eventually do not want to be controlled and it always backfires.

Research has shown that authoritarian parenting style is the least effective with the most detrimental results. Yet, most of us were parented that way, so we tend to lean on that style. In the flow of the Tao, we are allowing life to happen, not forcing it. However, this makes most of us uncomfortable. This is especially tricky when it comes to parenting, because there is a clear distinction between allowing life to flow and happen and not allowing our children to run wild. They do need boundaries, guidelines and to learn from life's natural consequences.

Being a conscious parent, we look for opportunities to provide choices, lessons and facilitate true life growth. We are not looking for the quick and easy fix (spanking, and punitive consequences) because they do not foster long-term learning and growth. They may stop the behavior in the moment, but the only lesson a child typically learns is that next time, they'll be trickier so they don't get caught.

We offer choices (we can live with): Do you want to lie quietly in your bed and sleep or do you want to lie quietly in your bed? Do you want to take a bath before or after dinner? Do you want to walk to your room or be carried? (If they throw themselves on the ground, "Oh, I see you'd like to be carried.") No brute force. Choices. Consequences, "Walls are not for coloring. Here is a magic eraser, let's see you make that disappear! When you are finished, I have paper on the table for coloring."

We are continually offering choices, and giving our child the opportunity to self-correct, learn and figure out how to do things differently. If we always "think" for them, they will never learn to think for themselves. This seems so obvious, yet when we are making decisions for them and doing for them what they can do for themselves that is precisely what we are doing.

31

Peace is the highest value. If you are not living in peace, how can you be content? The children are not the enemy. She doesn't want them to be harmed, nor is she happy when they fail. She enters the "battlefield" solemnly, as if she were attending a funeral.

Yea, this one is a bit somber. But, if we break it down, the truth is, if we are not living in peace, and we treat our children as the enemy, we are entering a battlefield, and it is sad. It doesn't need to be this way. We can choose differently to create peace in our homes and therefore contentment.

Ahh – this sounds good, but what does it *look* like? It looks like staying centered, staying "grounded", staying present and poised to do what needs to be done. We do this with the *intention* of being peaceful, creating a peaceful environment and showing our children what it looks like to choose peace. It is always a choice.

It does not look like conceding and giving in to every one of our child's whims, just to "keep the peace". It might often look like battle, which is when we enter it solemnly, however, the peace is what we keep within ourselves.

It would seemingly be more peaceful to not require our child to have a bedtime, for example. Many a war is waged over this. However, this is an important life skill (yes, skill – many people have not developed the self-discipline to get to bed on time and get adequate rest and no one functions well without the appropriate amount of sleep). Our job is to teach our child from an early age how to do this. When we set a schedule (preferably a visual schedule with times) that include, bath, snack, jammies on, teeth brushed, story (preferably a story told to by the parents with the ending left to the child to "dream up" and discuss in the morning), our child learns the importance of ritual and self-care.

No one wins with a shout-out, knock-down-drag-out fight. But, we can hold our ground and teach our children what it looks like to be at peace while moving through our lives.

We begin each "battle" with the question, "How can I have peace in this situation?" And move toward that.

32

You cannot see the Tao, yet in it, the whole world is contained. If everyone lived the Tao, we would live in harmony and the world would be a paradise. Laws would be unnecessary because people would carry it within their own beings.

The ultimate goal of parenting is to create whole people – a mensch is a Yiddish term for this. What this looks like is a person who carries "right and wrong" within their own being. They are not merely waiting for some authority to tell them what to do (or not), they have learned how to create and read their own moral compass. How many children today do what is right, but only when someone is looking? The challenge is in letting them learn and grow, while still creating healthy boundaries to move about and maintain their beautiful spirits.

It is a precarious balance of holding on and letting go. Kind of like when a child first learns to ride a bike. There are moments you hold on, to steady the bike, and then you let go. And yes, they might fall. You are there with loving, encouraging words to put them back on the bike and do it all again. It is a circular process that continues well into adulthood.

However, if we do not tell them "no" and help them integrate experiences into their lives, they will not ever learn to ride solo. There are many of adults today that have great difficulty in "riding solo" and suffer from a host of disorders and difficulties as a result.

We give our children choices and allow them to live with the consequences of these choices (especially when the consequences are small – going without a sweater at age 6 can be a valuable lesson in choosing the appropriate apparel and in the scheme of things the "suffering" minimal). As children grow, they assimilate these life-long lessons, so their ability to make choices (their "choice" muscle, so to speak) becomes stronger. They are learning that for every choice there is a consequence and that creates a stronger brain by which future choices can be reviewed, evaluated and appropriate choices made.

33

If you understand others, you are intelligent. If you understand yourself, you are enlightened. If you overcome others, you have strength. If you overcome yourself, you have authentic power. If we know we have enough, we are rich.

We spend a great deal of our lives learning about others. We spend very little time knowing who we are and developing our own true power. In parenting, our children will push all of our buttons and require us to "master" our own selves. When we realize we ARE enough, that we have all that we need, we truly are rich.

When we come from a place of being "full" as parents, we are not asking our children to fill us up. We do not ask them to live out our own dreams through their successes in academics, sports or even friendships. We do not require them to be our confidants or best friends. We do not seek their approval by buying them things or giving them things they are not ready for. We do not give in to all of their desires because we were not given things we wanted as a child and we are somehow assuaging our own inner hurts.

We "know" our children as their own beings, with their own soul agendas, and things to do here. We know them as separate from us. We know them as beautiful spirits who have chosen us to help them navigate through their lives to do what they have come here to do. We remain autonomous, yet connected. When we discipline and direct in love, we are seeing what we need to maintain our own healthy boundaries and what our child needs (which may vary from child to child, and age to age), in this moment. We drop into our heart centers and come from a place of unconditionally loving asking spirit, "What serves in this moment?"

We make constant contact with our own souls and "check in" and ask, "Who is this about" or "Who should own this problem?" We are conscious of what is ours and what is our child's. This is *true* enlightenment (as in living in light), strength and power.

34

The great Tao is like a flood – it can flow anywhere and everything comes from it, yet it does not create anything. It nourishes, yet lets go. It is one with all things as it is in the heart of all, hidden away and all things disappear into it, and it alone lasts. It does its work, but does not take credit for it. It is unaware of the magnitude of its greatness, thus it remains the greatest of all.

The Tao is synonymous to me with Great Mother, or Unconditional Love. Love gives birth to everything – it is the space from which all things come from, yet it doesn't "do" anything. It just is. It is "one" (whether we label what is happening good or bad) with everything, but it is at the heart of it all. When everything else goes away, the Tao is there. Love is there. It is constant and aware.

The goal of parenting, to me is to be a Divine Loving Presence from which all things birth themselves. When we create a space where Love is spoken (in words and deeds), where everyone is accepted for who they "be" exactly where they are at, who couldn't grow from there? Can you imagine being in the Presence where you were washed over with so much unconditional love? There is nothing that cannot be healed with that kind of Love.

When children "miss" behave, it is because they have somehow "missed" having one of their needs met. They have an inherent need, but may not know first, what that is and secondly, the appropriate way in which to get that need met. Part of that is the mixed messages we send. We say "do not lie", but when they tell us the truth, "I don't want to play with Suzy. She doesn't treat me well." And because Suzy is our best friend's daughter and we want them to be friends, we reply, "It's just a playdate. I'm sure you two can be friends." We have now taught them to "lie" about how they really feel, because we do not honor that feeling.

Can we teach our children how to identify their needs and healthy ways of getting those needs met? Can we love them through it by being able to hear (and see) some of the "ugly" thoughts and feelings? I know many households that do not allow the children to be angry. If the Tao is present in all things, it is present – even in anger. We can sit with it and allow it wash over, so that the underlying feelings of hurt can be expressed – reveal it, feel it, deal with it and finally heal it.

Love knows no limits. True love – unconditional Presence – the Tao is one with all things and all things will disappear into it – be swallowed up by its all-consuming Fire. And like the Phoenix, rising out of the ashes, what is no longer serving is gone and new life breaks forth out of the old.

35

Being centered in the Tao, you can go anywhere without harm. Even in pain, she sees harmony, for the Tao maintains peace within her own being. Words of the Tao seem flavorless, and you cannot see it, nor hear it. Yet it is endless in its supply.

The Tao is a space inside and all around that goes with us, making straight a crooked path and peaceful everything it passes through. The Tao is a clear space one creates within themselves that only seeks peace – like water seeking ground...it cannot help but find it. With clarity and precision, it sees only peace even in situations that are not peaceful. It accepts what *is* in the moment without question.

It seems flavorless – kind of like Tofu – which takes on the "flavor" of the thing it is paired with. The Tao, while maintaining its nourishing quality, will melt into what is there, yet providing what is necessary in the moment to make what is happening "whole", if we allow it. The problem is, we try to "see" what is happening with our senses...or "hear" words and not true meaning, or what is not spoken. Centered in the Tao, we can get underneath what is happening to the true heart of the matter, connecting with our child in the moment and looking beyond our senses. We look beyond the piercings, tattoos and colored hair, to a child that just wants to be "seen" and recognized for the individual that they are and loved unconditionally. We look beyond the child acting out in school to see with our heart, "What need is not being met?"

When we listen with our hearts and allow the Tao to be ever-present, we see beyond what is happening and healing can happen. Love will consume what is not serving and leave only the raw material by which we learn, love and grow. It is an endless supply, but we must connect to it and allow it to flow. We must be willing to look beyond what is happening in the moment to clearly see what is there.

When we do so, we might actually "see" our child clearly for the first time.

36

If you want to shrink, you must first expand. If you want to weaken something, at first it must be strong. The soft overcomes the hard. Let your work be done in secret, just show the results.

We learn about balance often when we are out of balance. We shrink after we have expanded and become weak, after we have been strong. This looks like being open to a new way of being and not using brute force to make things happen. We become soft, which overcomes the hard. When we work behind the scenes, no one knows what we do; they just see the results.

In parenting, sometimes we have to take a step back and allow our children the freedom to shrink and expand as they need to. Sometimes we have to allow them to show their own strength to find out where they are weak and still need to grow and learn. When we are soft and yielding, we can overcome the hard (thoughts, feelings, beliefs and unresolved places within us). We often find out what we want by first finding out what we do *not* want. It is like trying new recipes. We learn that too much salt can ruin a recipe and not enough leaves it bland and flavorless. Life, for children is all about assimilating all of the ingredients. As much as we would like to think our children learn from eating the cakes we serve them, it is the process of baking their own cake that they actually learn about life.

And you know what they say. If you're going to make a cake, you're going to have to crack some eggs. This is the process we all go through. We just forget when we become parents that our children need to experience most of life for themselves. Experience shapes the brain. Our children do not get nourished by the experiences *we* have, but by the richness of life they take in for themselves. Our job, if we were to label it, would be to provide wholesome ingredients and a great space for "mixing" it all up and trying it out. We also become the safe space for them to process when the cake tastes bad or doesn't rise. We get to listen and provide feedback or sometimes just be there to hold them and love them as they pick up the pieces and try again.

37

Centered in the Tao, in doing nothing, everything is done. If people were to center themselves in the Tao, they would be content and want for nothing. When there is no wanting, all things are at peace.

Our job, if there would be any, would be to work ourselves out of a job. At some point and time, we hope that these beings in our care would be able to traverse throughout their lives unencumbered. As we navigate with them, our goal is effortless effort. It is to arrive at the place where there is contentment and a "wanting for nothing".

We tend to be insatiable as human beings. We live in a time when many American children want for nothing. As a matter of fact, they are typically so overindulged that there never is a time that they do "want". Yet, they still do. This sense of wanting more and more does not create a very peaceful space.

How do we teach them this in a world of instant access to wait and to be content? To be still. To do "nothing" and allow things to happen. We do this by example. We live and allow them to watch as we take time for ourselves. We take time to stop and breathe and just "be" with life and each moment. Our children get their rhythms from us. We set the tone for being still and content. Are we continually hurried and rushed and do the words, "Hurry up" continually come out of our mouths? What can we let go of (in our schedules or our expectations) so that things can move more freely and effortlessly? The beautiful thing is that we get to make our own schedules and we get to decide if we want to be hurried or not. We just have to be aware when we are "not aware" in doing this.

In parenting, I used to think that I needed hours, if not days to spend with my children to "fill them up", and not having that, I would feel overwhelmed. I learned that little moments, even as little as five minutes of true connection can fill them right up. What tends to happen, is that the moments we spend are half-full - of us. When we can drop in, breathe deliciously deep into the moment to be with our child, drink them in, look deep into their sweet eyes, touch their heads, and "see" them, the "doing" is irrelevant. They "have us at hello" and that is all they truly need to be full.

38

The master goes deeper and looks at what is underneath, not what is "seen". She has no "will" of her own. She dwells in reality and lets all illusions go.

This verse speaks a lot to leaving things undone. In parenting there is so much "doing" and although things seem mostly and endlessly undone, this is a different kind of "undone". It is not doing – on purpose. We allow things to unfold without forcing our will, controlling the outcome or manipulating the situation so that we get what we want. Many of us, when we don't get what we want, use force to get it. We look for results – not what is brewing beneath the surface. We want things to be a certain way and usually try to move everything towards that end.

The Tao teaches us to look below the surface, to look at what is not seen. When we have no agenda, we can release what things "appear" to be and deal with what is happening.

In parenting, we often are looking at results (grades, behavior, messy rooms, etc.). We are not looking at what (or who) is behind all of these "illusions". What is the child in need of? Do we really "see" our children separate from us, with their own lives, soul growth to do, and paths to follow? Do we listen to what they are saying (or not saying) about who they are becoming?

When we can look beneath the surface, we can see the hurting child, the child that doesn't know how to express intense emotions or the child in need of boundaries and hearing the word "no". We look at the behavior and really see and understand what the language of the behavior is trying to communicate. When we go deeper and relinquish our will for what wants to happen, we will often find a buried treasure – our child opens their heart to us and we connect – sometimes for the very first time, True Self to True Self.

'Tis nothing sweeter than this.

39

When we are one with the Tao, everything moves in harmony, endlessly cycling. When we interfere, things become dirty, depleted and some even go away entirely. The Master sees all of the parts because she understands the "whole". She is humble and allows herself to be molded by the Tao.

In parenting, we often come off as the experts. We act as if we know the answers when in fact; we are fumbling through life very much like our own children, trying to figure it out as we go along. We make mistakes and if we are humble enough to be molded by the experience and learn and grow, we can flow effortlessly through life.

We tend to get locked into the part of our selves that want answers, that wants a concrete black or white answer and wishes to ensure (i.e., control) the outcome. When we get comfortable with the endless cycle, the coming and going, the birth, growth and dying of all things, we see that nothing is permanent and we can allow ourselves, and our children to be shaped and molded by life.

What we tend to do is bump up against it all with resistance. When our child makes a mistake, we focus on that instead of the lesson. When they come home with "bad" grades in middle school, we tend to punish, take things away or berate them for THEIR grades. We own problems that are not ours (our child's grades, their friendships, their school work, their extracurricular activities) and try to control the outcome. Our children do not learn responsibility by us being responsible for them or using punitive consequences. They learn by being given opportunities to be responsible and live with the natural consequences when they are not.

When we can see that life is cyclical and that we are continuously flowing in and out of these cycles, we can be less focused on results. This doesn't look like passivity. We still love, support, inquire, set boundaries and have guidelines for how we will be treated, but we take responsibility for what is ours and allow our children to do the same.

40

To yield – is the way of the Tao. All things come from nothing.

To truly surrender to the moment, each moment IS the Tao. It is an awareness of what is happening without resistance. There is no place to go, nothing to become, because you are already there. You ARE home. There is no place you can go but here. If you are struggling, you are home with the struggling. You drop the thoughts that are creating the *feelings* of struggling. As the Buddhist quote says, "Pain is inevitable. Suffering is optional."

How good are we at really "being" with the pain our children suffer without trying to fix it or talk them out of it ("Stop crying, you are o.k.")? Do we miss opportunities to teach responsibility by continually bailing them out?

In third grade, my daughter did not particularly like to read. She had specific reading goals (set by the school) to meet and there was a "dangling carrot" of a Popsicle promised by the teacher to the kids who met their goals. She took the tests on books she read, but wasn't motivated to read more, until she did NOT get the Popsicle. Tears flowed and pain erupted. I held her and really listened with compassion. I did not rescue her by continually reminding her of this "looming" goal prior to its arrival. She knew. Other parents took it upon themselves to "make" their children read, take the tests etc. I simply yielded, knowing this was her opportunity to learn and it was invaluable and although the stakes seemed high to her, in the scheme of things, this would be a "loss" she could overcome.

I sat with it and with her. I did not say, "I told you so" – the lesson was hers. I had compassion when I said, "It feels bad, I can see." This was her experience to learn and there would be no emails to the teacher to give her another chance, etc. In "being with what is", she learned something I could never have taught her.

By week 3 of the second quarter, she had surpassed her goal! Although I am not a fan of "dangling carrots", this was my child's experience and it was her choice to "own" it. Not mine.

All things come from nothing. Are we willing to "sit with" nothing until what wants to come, comes? Or do we choose to force our "will" or manipulate the situation for the desirable outcome?

41

The path towards "enlightenment" seems more like "in-dark-enment", to go forward, it seems you are going backwards, the straight path seems to take forever, "true power" appears weak...real clarity, seems "unclear" and authentic love seems indifferent and true wisdom seems child-like. The Tao cannot be found, yet it nourishes and completes all things.

I don't know about you, but in my 23 years of parenting experience, in walking towards "light", I have experienced a lot of "darkness". Not only has it felt that often I am walking and feeling my way through the dark without a clue, I have also experienced some darkened corners of myself that have come up to be looked at. When one lives in the Tao and parents this way, the light that the Tao brings into each situation can often expose darkened corners within us that need to be looked at. This can often feel like we are going backwards and as we give up control, we can feel very "weak" as we learn our True Selves and the connection to authentic Power.

Often the "rules" become unclear as we learn to listen to ourselves and the underlying unconditional Loving Presence that we are tapping into. It doesn't often look like what we are used to seeing and when we truly love, it would appear "indifferent" – non-attached to the outcome (what!? I don't have to be invested in my child's grades, success, friendships, piano performance and/or baseball career?) It might appear to others that we do not "care" or do not "love" our child when we step back and allow them to own their own grades and we do not put them into every afterschool activity known to man, or "push" them to do better, achieve more, or "polish" off that book report project (after all, other parents do their kids' assignments).

When we are "wise" we become like little children in that we believe in all things and we relinquish the need to "know it all" and control all outcomes. We allow life to flow for ourselves, and our children and we guide them, but we step back when they need us to and move in with love when they need our love and support. The Tao cannot be found...it is invisible, without a clear description, yet when we are in it, when we are flowing from a place that has zero expectations, that truly loves what comes up – even in its darkest form, we have never felt so light.

This is the "beam" that lights up the path for our child to follow.

42

Most people hate to be alone. But the Master – she knows how to use this, to love it and realize she is never alone, for she is One with all that is.

Parenting, even if you have a partner, can feel like a "lone" journey. We spend a lot of time processing the experiences of parenting if we are conscious. If we are unconscious, we spend a lot of time repeating patterns of our childhood (whether they worked or not) and regurgitating things from our past. We spend very little time in solitude, trying to look underneath it all.

We are a society of treating symptoms. There are thousands of books that deal with "behavior" or more specifically "mis-behavior". Which is an interesting concept. In the adult world, if someone does not have an optimal experience, we don't call it misbehavior. We only do this with children. What it is - is a lack of understanding or ability to have a need met. We all have inherent needs and when these are not met, we try different strategies to meet them or escape them.

Children are no different. If they are "screaming" for attention in some way, they are asking to be truly seen, heard, validated and mostly unconditionally loved. This does not mean that we tolerate all behaviors. It DOES mean we stop and connect to what is underneath the behavior. We take the time to ask ourselves, "What is my child trying to communicate with this?" When we are parenting in the Tao, we are conscious of not only what is happening, but the "why". What is the intention – what is the need (is it physical – are they tired, hungry, sick, poorly nourished, or have an undiagnosed allergy?), or is it emotional (are the sad, angry, frustrated, scared?) or is it mental (are they on overload, in over the heads, booked with so many activities that they have no downtime?), is it spiritual (do they have a connection to something bigger than themselves, do they know how to breathe deep and meditate and calm themselves down and ask for help when the need it?)

When we drop into solitude, we are able to connect with our Inner Wisdom that guides and directs us toward solutions – not quick fixes. We can swiftly and with clarity move into heal – not just bandage. Sometimes there are deep wounds that need to be healed...within us AND our child. If we are willing to take the time to be quiet, the healing can occur. We just have to listen – with our hearts.

43

Gentle ways overcome the hard, unmovable ways. When something has no "form" it can enter – even when there is no space. When we teach without using any words at all and "do" without doing, this is the Master's way...the Way of the Tao.

We teach our children most by what we do *not* say, and what we do *not* do. If only 7% of what we communicate is with words, wow...there is a lot of "saying without saying." Do our children feel our unconditional love? Or do they feel our frustration with them, our disappointment (even if these words are not spoken) or our intolerance of their child-like ways? Do our "words" match our behaviors and are we moving into spaces our child leaves open with love and grace?

We when take our 2-year-old into a nice restaurant without anything to do, and become exasperated because the child does not sit still, we are parenting unconsciously. We are expecting behaviors from a child that are not remotely possible. When we are gentle, we are continually flowing with what is happening and consciously aware of what we are teaching. We can "do without doing" because there is nothing to "do". We simply become comfortable with Being in the Flow and moving into right action – whatever that looks like in the moment because we have cleared out what we *think* should happen.

However, in doing so, we must clearly look at ways in which we have become "hard" and un-moveable. When we expect things from our children that are not within their ability to do, we are not flowing with the Tao. We are resisting "what is" and this creates a great deal of frustration for all concerned.

What this looks like in the above scenario is planning ahead...if you *need* to go out late with the children for dinner, you can call ahead and order the food, so that when you sit down, it is ready. We used to have a restaurant only bag, in the trunk, with paper, crayons, stickers – fun games, hand-held etch-a-sketch and the water doodle pad, so when we were caught unprepared, we had something to fall back on. Schedule dinner early. When our son was in the throes of autism, it was difficult to go out. We would often arrive separately and one of us would order ahead of time. We could enjoy some amount of "normalcy" but we had to be realistic about our expectations and be willing to make conscious adaptations based on our situation to ensure that we were able to live in peace.

It's not perfect all the time, but when we are parenting on purpose and consciously, we are always looking at the "Tao" flowing through. How can I do this with ease and grace and accept "what is" while continually looking at ways in which I am resisting what is actually happening? How can I set healthy boundaries for myself and my children and allow them to realize the consequences of their choices while loving them, supporting them and guiding them when appropriate? We don't go on autopilot. We become "soft" by being continually open to change, to grow, and able to be with what is happening.

44

Be content where you are, with what you have and what you are able to do. Be happy with the way things are. When you finally "get it" – that there is nothing missing – the whole world opens up and you own the entire world!

Ahh...being content. It seems there is always "more" to learn, more to have, be and do. We live in a world that is continually in upgrade mode. A new iPhone is available before you have finished downloading all the new apps for the current one. One thing we have forgotten to program into our lives is the life app that we are *already* enough in need of no new downloads. What we are in need of often is just a reboot.

In doing so, we agree to relinquish all the programming we have carried around that is no longer serving us. Our "motherboard" is in serious need of an overhaul.

If we continually compare ourselves with other parents, we might feel that we are not enough. In living with the Tao, we settle into the peaceful place that we *are* enough - that we *have* enough and that we *do* enough. We are happy with how things are and we open up to the whole world. When we connect with this vibrating and pulsating energy, the answers arise of their own accord. What we seek, seeks us and better yet, finds us. We are able to stop all the doing and drop into "being" – the witness who sees without judgment what is playing out on the stage of our lives. From the behind-the-scenes vantage point, we see what is happening, but we are not drawn into the drama. We witness with clarity and from this place, we act.

The Tao is the Writer/Director of the play and allows the drama to unfold, but recognizes the ability to influence change but only if she does not get caught up in the illusion. How do you do this? You stay centered by quieting the mind each day and connecting to Source – whatever you call it. It's the "mother ship" that has endless energy and wisdom that we can tap into and infinite possibilities and resources. We have access to endless information when we open up this connection. When we take into this space our concerns, "seeming" problems (and I say "seeming" as they are merely misperceptions of the situation that need a realignment with Truth), and difficulties, we can find clarity, peace and the entire world of answers and resources are available to us.

We have to create a time, a space (open, clear and willing heart) to listen. If we do what we've always done, we'll get what we've always gotten. If we stop, step back, look and listen in the clear, quiet moment, we will download the right and perfect answer. It often surprises us, as it is already contained with us. It is the Tao. It is love. It is clarity. It is peace. It is.

45

Great perfection seems flawed and fullness can seem empty but it is fully aware. When something is truly straight, it can look "crooked" and sometimes real wisdom seems silly. The Master can allow things to happen and plays with things as they come, getting out of the way, she allows the Tao to speak through her – often without words.

Have you ever looked at a child's drawing? Have you ever seen it, really seen their artwork through their eyes. Can you see the wonder, the magic – the possibility and the absolute pure way in which it is absolutely perfect – yet might not make any "sense" at all? Have you ever been so full – so happy that it could not be contained...thus it was "empty" as in not needing to be any fuller than it is or simply no ability to contain it? Sometimes when we are living in the Tao – it might appear to others that we are meandering down a path that has no real direction. Yet, when we are willing to take what is offered and play with it, get out of the way of it, it flows effortlessly and we are always right where we need to be.

This looks like loving without conditions. This feels like giving away what we want to be given. When our child is cranky, whiny and all over the place, they represent pieces of us and we can get what we so desperately need in that moment, if we give it away. If we give, compassion, patience, simplicity with our words and deeds, we get to heal us both. I really believe that is what the golden rule is,"Do unto others as you would have them do unto you." As in...YOU do it first. Give away what you want from them and what you want for yourself.

Our children do not learn compassion from terse, angry words. Our children do not learn patience from being hurried. Our children do not learn tolerance from our unrealistic expectations and intolerance of their miss-takes. They do not learn kindness and love when we are continually letting them know how they can "improve" themselves.

They learn to give back what we give them. They learn to be loving by being loved. They learn to be respectful by being respected. They learn to be responsible by having responsibility handed to them. They learn to "be" when we allow ourselves to "be" lived...by the Tao.

There is an ancient form of art, finding the beauty in the transient and imperfect called Wabi Sabi. There are no real words to sufficiently describe it, because it is more of a feeling or way of being. The famous tea master, Sen no Rikyu of Kyoto used this concept when he constructed a tea house with a very low door so that even an emperor had to bow to enter...to remind everyone of the importance of humility. Wabi Sabi is finding the beauty or the "art" in imperfection. We adopt the mind-set of meditating on knowing – and not knowing, on existing and not existing and then we leave both behind so that we just might "be". Being allows the Tao to be lived through us. "Imperfections" and all.

46

There is no greater illusion than fear and nothing worse than walking through life prepared to fight against an "enemy". If you can see through your fear, you will always be safe.

Fear is such a great motivator that it has been used forever as a way to control. We fear war, so we stockpile weapons, we fear being taken advantage of, we purchase a gun, we fear "loss", we purchase insurance, we fear lack of control, we create laws and religion. Punishment is all fear driven. The problem with relying on fear in parenting is that you actually trigger physical responses that impede your child's ability to learn from you. When a child is stressed, cortisol is released. High cortisol levels can damage brain cells in the hippocampus, which plays a major role in memory and learning. No one learns when they do not feel safe. Their biological response (fight, flight or "freeze") kicks in and the child is immobilized.

When we use fear, our children begin to get the feeling they are not "good enough" and this sense of powerlessness can result in power struggles. We want to invoke intrinsic motivation and a sense of cooperation with the world. This is especially important as children grow and hit adolescence. If they have always been parented with fear – or dangling carrots (good or bad), their motivation will always be outside of them. Guess who they look to when they are no longer looking to you? Yes, they look to their peers.

When we give choices, when we stop operating in fear, everyone gets to feel safe and there is no greater environment for learning, growing and "being" than that.

When we peer through fear (ours and our child's), we see love and we are safe. We are being lived by the Tao and when we trust in this, we are free from our greatest enemy.

47

The further one goes out into the world, the less they understand. The Master gets everywhere without going anywhere, can see without looking and in doing nothing, achieves everything.

This sounds a lot like magic or wizardry, doesn't it? How is it possible to accomplish everything without doing anything? It all depends on what it is you are intending to accomplish. Very often, when asked what people want for their children, they will say for them to be "happy". When asked what qualities they would like to instill in their children, they are things like, love, kindness, goodness, success and responsibility. Yet, very often we are not doing anything to ensure these things happen. We are powering our way through parenting with a checklist of things to do and accomplishments for our child to achieve without stepping back and seeing how are we *actually* providing opportunities for the qualities to be learned and assimilated?

Dr. Stuart Brown is the founder of The National Institute of Play. He has studied animals in the wild. What he has observed over 20 years is that animals "play" in order to discover things about themselves, find out how they are safe, hone their skills and learn intrinsic qualities about their world and other animals. This "play" can often look like missed-behavior, if equated to human behavior. When we are observing our children and the ways in which they are learning, they are communicating what they are learning, trying out boundaries, finding ways to get their needs met, learning what works (for them and others) and what doesn't. They learn how to regulate their own behaviors to get what they need and also how that fits in with those around them.

When we are looking to instill all of the wonderful qualities our children need to "be happy", we must look at *how* we are doing this. It is through the minutia – the ways we talk to our children when they are tired, hungry, angry, frustrated and have "missed-behaviors". This is when we are the most effective. This is when we get to teach the most about compassion, tenderness, kindness and unconditional love. These are the moments of true learning, where we *give away* the qualities we want to foster in ourselves and instill in our children.

48

When we are learning, each day we add something. When we practice the Tao, every day we let something go. We stop forcing things until we finally settle into not acting at all. Then, when nothing is done – there is nothing that needs to be done. True Mastery comes from letting things be and not interfering.

If there is even a 10% chance that your child will be able to solve the problem they have in front of them, would it not be wise to do nothing and see what happens? We are so quick to rush in – just right before the moment they are figuring it out. How often do we do for them, what they could do for themselves, if we just had the patience to let go and "wait for it". In dealing with my son's autism, I learned that with his delayed processing, we had to slow down our world a lot. He could not nor would not be hurried - into anything. I learned to stop and wait. I learned when I asked him a question, I would need to not only wait for him to process the question, but wait for the answer. It was often so tempting to provide the answer for him. But, he didn't learn from this, so I waited.

When we let go in our parenting, we can let things be (beds get made imperfectly, assignments are not always letter-perfect, shoes get tied slower, messes are made, time passes), and not always interfere. When we see them struggle, if we can take a breath, and communicate (mostly without words) our faith in them and our belief that they have all they need to accomplish the task at hand, we allow them to add knowledge while releasing any beliefs that they cannot do it. Self-efficacy is an innate belief that "I can do anything!" This has been proven to be necessary for healthy self-esteem and fostering self-worth. Our children can only gain this knowledge by being allowed to do things without our interference and with our unconditional love and support. This is true Mastery. For both us, and our children.

49

The Master is true goodness in that she is good to those who are "good" and to those who are "not good" and she trusts those who are trustworthy and those who are not. She believes in those who believe and in those who do not believe. Her mind is empty - like space, and she is rarely understood. People look to her and she treats them like her own.

The Master sits right in the middle where good and bad are equal distances apart. Without the judgment, she can be with what "is" without having to impart any kind of opinion about it one way or another. She can trust anyone, because trust is housed within her – not outside of her. She is open, which is why people come to her. Holding a "space" for someone to come where there is no judgment or where you can feel completely safe regardless of what you think or what you have done is the most conducive for healing. Most of us only experience this space during therapy.

In parenting, it is helpful if we can step back from our own judgments and ask ourselves, "How do we create balance and harmony within ourselves and then give that away to our children?" Ultimately, our children will not learn what we teach them, but they will learn what we have lived-out in front of them. When they feel that when they are with us, they get to reset to what the middle way is, because that is where we live, they can only live a life that is balanced. When we take time to breathe, meditate and truly enjoy our lives, we teach them the same.

I received too much money back at Wal-Mart once. I had asked for $20 back, but the guy accidentally gave me $50. It was wrapped up in my receipt, and in a hurry, I didn't notice until I returned home. It was late, the kids were hungry and so I called the store and told them I would return it the next day. When I went to return the money, they did not have a "policy" in place and did not know what to do because no one had ever returned money before and we had to wait for twenty minutes while they figured it out. My kids were witness to all of this and although, in the scheme of things, "it really didn't matter", it mattered to me and it mattered to them. Our children are scanning everything we do and uploading it as ways of being in this world. Being "true goodness" is what we want to emulate even if doesn't seem to matter or if others do not understand our action.

50

The Master gives herself to the moment. She knows each moment will die and she will have nothing left to hold onto. There will be no more illusions, no more resistance and she doesn't think of her actions as they flow from WHO she is. She holds nothing back from life and is ready for death when it comes, like a good night's sleep after a hard day's work!

Each moment we are dying, in one form or another and often in multiple ways at once. We let go of so many things throughout our lives that when we finally "get it" we know that we truly hold nothing. It all goes away. What we end up doing is trying to grab air, control it and hold onto it. When we relinquish the control, all things flow easily from us – because they are not ours and never were.

When we begin to see our children as fellow-travelers, we become less concerned about the outcome, about controlling what they do, and more focused on our connection with them, our interactions and the intentions behind the "doing". We can let them own their experiences and we get to "sideline" with them about it. They are more apt to listen and appreciate what we have to say when they sense we are always rooting for them, love them unconditionally and have 100% faith in their ability to figure it out.

Can you imagine what you would be able to "do" if you knew at the core of who you were that "who you be" was enough? Ah, even more than enough and life was perfect and exactly as you created it to be in order to do what you came here to do.

It is our jobs (if we were to give ourselves one) to remind our children of who they are so that THEY can figure out what they came to do. As we hold up mirrors of their perfect, Divine Self, they get to see the reflection of their own divinity in our eyes.

51

Everyone is part of the Tao. It becomes "conscious" of itself through us and allows circumstances to complete it. The Tao gives birth to all things and nourishes them, sustains them and cares for them as it takes all beings back into itself. It creates without owning, it acts without concern for results, guides without intruding and is the very nature of all things.

The Tao/Life/Love becomes conscious of itself through us. We are the physical, tangible ways in which it is expressed. However, we are often so concerned with what we are doing, that we are unaware of what is wanting to be birthed through us. As we parent our children, we can become aware of our own patterns that are blocking the flow. Where are we not allowing what we want to give away to our children to actually come *in* to us?

If we want to exude patience and give that to our children, how can we allow it to flow to us first? If we want to nourish them, are we allowing nourishment into our own lives? If we want to have a calmer and peaceful interaction with our child, are we having that same calm and peaceful interaction in our own heads? Sometimes our children just state the obvious or that which we ourselves are feeling but do not feel we should articulate.

We cannot change it if we are not aware of it. Becoming aware – becoming "conscious" of whether or not we are conscious, is the first step in doing so.

Then, as we settle into nurturing and caring for ourselves, what we give away is what is inside. The Tao is truly conscious of itself through us because it is what we have become.

52

All things begin with the Tao and return to it. When we know the Mother of the world, we know the children. When we are free of judgment and our senses, we live in peace. When we are able to see into the dark, the way is clear. When we know how to yield, we become strong, connecting to The Source of light, we use our own light.

The Tao, like the silence between notes, the pause between words, the space between breathing out and breathing in, is the nothingness from which all possibilities come into being. When we find ourselves in this space, everything becomes clear. We can peer through the "dark", because we are no longer using our senses. The Light we carry within shines into the darkness. Much of parenting, let's face it, is filled with darkness. Not in a sense that anything is "wrong", but because the answers are not always clear and our kids certainly do not come with a manual.

We are making it up as we go along and we have learned to rely on our senses. One sense we do not pay as much attention to is our sixth sense, or the part of us that "knows without knowing". This only comes to us when we are in the Tao, the space in between, the "nothingness". When we live in balance, we can easily go one way or the other with fluid grace. It's like riding in the middle lane down the freeway, going left or right is always an option.

What we hope to recognize in our children is their innate goodness. The essence of who they are versus our concepts about who they should be (or who we think they already are). Do they have the freedom to move freely outside of the lines we have drawn for them? If we recognize it, do our children know that we do and do we communicate (with words and deeds) that they are inherently good, beautiful, perfect and unconditionally loved?

Do we know how to yield?

53

The way of the Tao is easy, yet most people prefer the side paths. Become aware of being out of balance, finding center in the Tao. When we are out of balance, as a nation we focus on things and not on what matters.

In keeping with the Tao, we maintain a sense of equilibrium so that when our children swing from one end to the other, they have a point of reference to return "home". We know ourselves through our extremes and as children learn and grow, they will push boundaries, play around with what is theirs to do and try out all kinds of side paths. We all do. We learn to turn the light on when it is dark. It is when we are motivated the most to find light that we actually seek it.

We generally seek it outside of ourselves. We find it in others first, but when we finally come "home" we recognize it within our own being. When we "live" here, we live in the Tao, in a state of balance. When we parent from here, we understand that our children must find this place for themselves, which means they won't inherently know where it is and might need to try out behaviors that can "miss" the mark, on occasion. But, if we maintain OUR balance, centered, clear, and loving, we can be a beacon as to what that light looks like. We cast out our light into their shadows with words of encouragement and love, not chastising and fear.

I have never found anyone to be talked out of their "fear" or operating from this place by telling them "not to be afraid." We relinquish our fears when we have something better to hold onto. That is where our love comes in. When I asked a group of children I work with, "Who is afraid that there is a monster under their bed?" They all raised their hands. When I asked them if any of them had ever found one, none of them raised their hands. Yet, they were still afraid. Sometimes our fears are irrational and do not make sense. But first, we connect with our child, where they are at (their fear) with an understanding of what it is like to be afraid, "It can be scary to think those things." Then, we offer a "bridge" to a different thought, "I know when I have fearful thoughts, it makes me feel very scared." Then, we can take them to a new thought, "But, I remind myself that I am safe and protected. What would make you feel safe and protected right now?"

It's like a good phone conversation. Dial up. Establish the connection. Speak to what the child is actually saying. And then you "end" with some type of closure (hug, snuggle time, or just a heart-to-heart connection).

It all starts when we become aware when things are out of balance. Usually, this is within us.

54

That which is well established cannot be uprooted. When our roots go deep into the Tao, we will never be rooted up. Cultivate it in yourself, your family, your community, in the country and in the world and it will prosper. To be "real" one must embrace the Tao. How do we know this? We look inside ourselves.

Roots are interesting thing. We talk about them when we talk about our families – our "roots". I grew up in a small town called "Rootstown". It is ironic, because I have had anything but roots since I left there as I have moved over 15 times in the last 20 years! But it does speak to me about where do we hook in or more importantly to what do - we connect to that gives us the ability to branch out.

There's a great song out right now titled, "Roots Before Branches" and the lyrics state, "I've gotta have roots before branches...know who I am before I know who I'm gonna be..." Our parenting provides the roots by which our children plant themselves so that they might grow. What are we guiding them to root themselves in?

When we make them dependent upon us by telling them what to do, how to think and manipulating the environment for them, we teach them to rely on us. When we do this, we operate out of fear. I believe we all inherently know we are connected (as in "rooted") in something greater than ourselves. Yet often, we do not practice this on a regular basis. We might "plug-in" on Sundays, but then the rest of the week, we rely solely on ourselves.

As we parent consciously, we look to root ourselves in Truth, to connect to our Divine Nature and "plug-in" daily (if not continually) to our Source. As we do that, we become a conduit by which our children connect as well. When they see us rooted in Truth, in the Tao, they can also feel the peaceful unmovable space we reside in and from which all of our decisions spring forth. Our life becomes a series of responses springing forth from our core, not knee-jerk reactions to what is happening at the moment. It is as if there is a continual strand of Truth and Love that guides our every action that is connected to the Ultimate Truth.

When we root ourselves in this – our branches reach up towards the heavens and the "fruit" we bear is oh-so-very sweet!

55

When we are in harmony with the Tao, we become like a baby – with bones that are soft, muscles that are weak – but a powerful grip. The Master is powerful in that she lets all things come and go – effortless effort – wanting nothing. She never expects results and is therefore never disappointed. Thus, her spirit never grows old.

When we parent in harmony with the Tao, we are supple, like a newborn in that we are so flexible and bendable. Yet, the "grip" we have on life is so anchored – it is incredibly powerful. With effortless effort, we glide through parenting because we do not have an agenda. We do not expect results, therefore we cannot be disappointed.

What does this look like, you ask? Should we not "expect" our child to do well in school? Should we not expect them to pick up their clothes, be responsible, respectful and successful? There is a difference between setting the intention and fostering an environment that naturally evokes respect and cooperation and demanding that a child do all of the above. Most of us parent from fear which demands ("If you do not do "X", "Y" will happen." Or "You got all "F's on your report card, you are grounded.") When we live in harmony, we are flowing with what is.

We respect ourselves and our children by setting boundaries and providing appropriate guidance. Such as: appropriate bedtimes, times and an environment to do homework (which might mean less activities), adequate rest time availability, healthy snacks, spiritual guidance (by way of our examples), quality family time, age-appropriate responsibilities (picking out their own clothes, getting themselves up in the morning, making their own lunch, doing their own laundry at a certain age, helping with dinner, being responsible for their own homework by middle school, etc.). When these things are cultivated in an environment that is kind, respectful, and unconditionally loving, we need not expect results. We simply plant the seeds and watch them grow. When the soil we have planted in is rich, and we continually water it and provide sunshine – they cannot help but grow into all they can be.

We don't need to "control" the environment, "If you don't go to sleep right now, there will be no TV tomorrow." We respect the child (and ourselves) with an appropriate boundary. We can say, "Your body needs at least 9 hours of sleep for your age. You need to get up by "X" time. Therefore, this is the appropriate bedtime." The child might say, "I don't wanna sleep!" To which we can say, "I cannot make you sleep. But, I do need to provide you the right amount of time to do so. So, you can rest quietly in your bed and sleep or just rest quietly in your bed. What is your choice?"

No expectations. We don't have to be angry, because we aren't looking for results. We set up boundaries, and we teach our child that they have choices and the ability to decide for themselves (within age-appropriate ranges) what they need. They "practice" good decision-making and learn from their "missed-takes" and accumulate this knowledge (as in create deep and strong roots) for more difficult decision-making circumstances in the future.

If we are always making their decisions, how will they ever learn? What then, are they rooted in when they need to make major decisions in their lives?

56

Those who know, don't talk. Those who talk don't know. When we close our mouths, turn off our senses, relax and soften our glares, we return to our original Selves. The Tao gives itself up continually, which is why it lasts forever.

As parents, we tend to talk *way* too much! We are constantly explaining, re-explaining and bargaining with our children. I am not saying that a solid explanation isn't necessary. I think it is important for our children to understand why we set bedtimes (they need adequate rest), why they have responsibilities, etc. But, when we are in the line at the grocery store and negotiating and explaining 10 times our decision, we are wasting our breath.

Our Original Self knows the answer. When we speak it should be clear, precise and our actions should back-up what we are saying. If we have explained to our child that they cannot have candy (it is close to dinner or whatever), we should not have to explain 10 more times. Mostly, we get worn down and we give in and that is why our children keep pushing us. I am not saying that an occasional, "Hmm...I have thought about this again, and I think it would be o.k. today to do that. It's fun to have a treat now and then, huh?" When we parent on purpose, and consciously, we are aware of what we do, why we do it and how we do it.

Yet, we understand and take into consideration our child's age, their abilities, their understanding of the world and that they are trying to have their needs met with limited knowledge of how to do that. We understand that they are continually reorganizing their brains in order to become more efficient and might "forget" or need to re-learn concepts as they grow in an understanding of how these things relate to them.

We give ourselves up continually to the process of thinking we know what our child is going through and drop into the space where we attune with our child so that we get a better understanding of where they are coming from. When we do this, we can close our mouths and connect with our True Self, which guides us to the Truth and bonds us with our child's innate goodness.

57

If you want to be a great leader, in learning to follow the Tao, you stop trying to control and you let go of your plans and allow the world to be as it is. The more you prohibit, the less intrinsically motivated people are, the more weapons, the less secure and the more you help when it is unnecessary, the less people learn to rely on themselves. When we can let go of our desire for the common good, the "good" becomes common, for each takes responsibility for his or herself.

I have been reading and "working" with the Tao for most of my life, but the past 6 years, I have read the Tao te Ching each day and have assimilated it over time. What I have learned (or rather unlearned) is to relinquish the illusion of control. I have never been in control...I had just created a very believable illusion that this was the case. In letting go of my plans, the plans that wanted to come forth (and quite frankly, they didn't always make logical sense to me!) came into fruition. With a continual trust in "what was", I was able to just allow.

In parenting, it is very difficult to not "control". We are in charge of and responsible for these precious beings and without our doing for them when they are infants, they would die. It is a very difficult transition for us to go from being completely responsible for them to their being responsible for themselves. However, if we do not, at some point start transferring the "power", they will not be able to be responsible for themselves.

The tricky part is when and what. In working with the developmentally delayed population there is a conundrum of when to help and when to step back. There is a phenomenon called "learned helplessness". This is a condition by which a person will fail to help themselves, even when they are fully capable, and in doing so will either gain a reward or even avoid an unpleasant consequence. We can often unknowingly do this to our children. We incapacitate them by doing for them what they are able to do for themselves.

When we parent consciously, we must continually ask ourselves, "Is there the remote possibility that my child can figure this out for themselves?" If not, can we scaffold (as in provide the minimal help or intervention) for success? This does NOT look like tying their shoes for them, making their breakfast or lunch for them after a certain age. This looks like teaching them skills and responsibility along the way so that they can "do it themselves." When we do this, we let go and allow them to learn in their own way, their own timing and often how "not" to do something is as important as how to do it.

This can often take longer, be messier and require we drop our concept of how it needs to be done. They might discover a better way for themselves. Stepping back and allowing the learning is the most difficult part for us because it requires us to let go of our desire for the common good. It's not that our ideas aren't good and wholesome and helpful. They are just *our* ideas. Our child needs to come up with their own.

58

When a country (or children) are presided over with acceptance, they are comfortable and honest. When they are repressed, they become sullen and manipulative. When you try to make them happy, you set them up to be miserable. The Master serves as an example and does not impose her will. She is pointed without piercing, straightforward, yet flexible, and radiates from within.

The original translation is "tolerance" and although this is an adequate word, I prefer the word acceptance. I myself do not simply want to be tolerated. In our country, tolerance is a great goal. With our children, we want to broaden the word to acceptance. When children are accepted for who they are and where they are at, they feel comfortable, at ease and can be honest about their experiences. They can easily tell you when they have done something that feels "wrong" because they are accepted and your love shines through to help them self-correct and make changes, not shame, blame and punish.

When we are continually "trying" to make them happy, we are imposing our idea of happiness upon them without allowing them to figure out what this looks like for themselves. When we live our own truth, following our own bliss, our children get to watch and learn what it looks like to live and stand in truth. When they continually witness us being calm, centered, peaceful – even amidst some stormy weather, they see that our words do in fact, match our deeds.

We become clear about who we are and are independent of others' opinions and we move forward fearlessly, yet are flexible in our thinking. We can encourage our children by noticing what seems to provide them joy or evokes sadness. "I noticed when you are painting a picture, your whole face lights up." Or "I noticed whenever you come home from "X's" house, you seem sad." We are straightforward, yet we have no attachment to the outcome...we are merely helping articulate and reflect what our child might not be conscious of themselves. Then, we step back and allow them to do with it what they would like.

Try starting sentences with, "I noticed... or hmm...it seems to me...or I just observed this and wanted to check in with you..." we honor what we see and "dial up" to make the connection and see if this is resonating with them, too. We then step back to support them in the process of handling it.

59

The mark of a moderate (woman) is freedom from her own ideas. She makes use of anything life throws at her. She moves like a tree in the wind. Nothing is impossible because she has let go.

Life throws lots of stuff at us. Probably the reason there is no real parenting manual is that there is no "one size fits all". There are so many circumstances and possibilities that it would be impossible to cover each one. Not to mention that all children are so different. Yes, there are some inherent similarities. But I know with the five children who have been in my care, they each require (and have each excavated) something slightly different from me.

When we parent, free from our own ideas, it does not mean that we don't have any ideas. We are just not attached to them. Sometimes, as parents we get so locked down in our ways – we have an idea about how things HAVE to be and we are no longer supple. We parent the way we were parented, often by default. We don't move like a tree in the wind – we become more like iron fences. Very, very "good" parents, who only want what is best for their children often forget to include their children in their decisions. What I mean by that is that they make choices for them, "for their own good" but the question is, at a certain age (and I'm talking adolescence here), if they are not "buying it" – how invested do you think they are going to be in your decision?

Choosing our child's clothes, friends, classes at school or school itself, beyond a certain age, even though it might be in their best interest, if they are not "interested", they will not invest. At some point, we have to be "free from our own ideas" at least long enough to entertain that our growing budding children (who have come through us, not TO us), have ideas of their own. When we sit with our children and listen to them...with our hearts...they truly are pretty self-explanatory. We also have to ask ourselves, why am I so invested in these things?

Nothing, including parenting, is impossible, if we can let go. Control is not something we all give up easily. But, if we understand it is a mere illusion, anyway – what is there to really give up?

60

Parenting (or governing, as this translation says) is like frying a small fish – you can ruin it with too much poking. When you are centered in the Tao, "bad" has no power. Not that it doesn't show itself, but when you are clear, you see it and are able to get out of its path. When you give what is bad nothing to oppose (by labeling things "good or bad"), it disappears into itself.

Ah...we poke a lot as parents. "Sit up straight, did you brush your teeth, where is your homework, why are your shoes in the middle of the floor, did you feed the cat, who borrowed my scissors and didn't return them, you are wearing *that,* I'm sure you want to wear this, eat your broccoli..." and on and on we poke.

We poke, because we have been poked. It is what we know and it "seems" to be a way in which we demonstrate our "caring," our "loving," and "taking care of".

But mostly, it *feels* like poking.

Imagine going to lunch with a dear friend. You meet him or her and the first thing they say is, "Wow, *what* did you do to your hair?" (in a not-so-approving fashion), and they continue throughout the conversation to point out ways in which you do not "measure up" or ways in which you can "improve" upon yourself.

About how long would that lunch last?

Yet, we do this to our children all the time. It is not that these things do not necessarily need to be said. But, can we say them differently, less or can we sandwich it in there with lots of love and acceptance?

Playfulness is a great way to do this. When we play with our kids, we teach them to laugh at life, with life and to not take things so seriously. Life already shows up that way. Why not take the "sting" out of it, by being more playful?

We can "play" with the seemingly bad, "I see the teacher agrees with me. I see an "F" – for FANTASTIC...yet, I'm noticing you are struggling with these math problems...how can I help?" and provide necessary tutoring, assistance, etc. Your child hasn't picked up their room in days. "Play" with it...send a paper airplane in with a note..."Is a rescue necessary? I cannot see the floor...wondering if everyone survived the hurricane in there?" Offer to break down the task into manageable steps, if it seems overwhelming – like, "I'll grab the dirty clothes for you and then you'll be able to have room to put the other stuff away".

We can always ask, "How would I like to be treated in this situation?" We get to give away what we want to receive (and funny...as our children grow up that is *exactly* what happens! Regardless of what it "is" we have given them -"good or bad", it comes back to us).

When we oppose nothing...as in, we are able to accept things as they are; we look carefully at what is going on. We ask ourselves, "Whose problem is it anyway?" Quite frankly, kids can live in messes. I was a horribly messy child and adolescent. I had absolutely NO problem with it! Waging war over a clean room is ridiculous. Think about it, if something causes YOU that much stress – fix it. If not, let it go. Work on a middle ground. Our agreement at our house was, once a week – the floor would be vacuumed, which meant all of the life-forms had to be off of the floor first! Food eaten in rooms would be taken to the kitchen nightly (this after an ant infestation...urgh!).

If I don't want something there, *I* pick it up and move it. I clearly own "my problem" and deal with it. If I want assistance, I can point it out – but, I must be clear that it is my issue and not wage war and try to "control" the situation. I will only waste *my* brain cells and *my* good energy getting all heated up about it. When I call it "bad", it is so and I can choose to get out of its way. When I call it "good", I can own that too. The "Truth" about it – is it just "is".

If you want to test this theory, ask any teenager what a "clean" room is. Then ask an adult (specifically a Mom).

"Truth" is relative.

61

Great power is like the sea, all streams run towards it. When a great woman makes a mistake, she realizes it. When she does, she admits it, corrects and considers those who point out her mistakes her teachers. Her "enemies" are mere shadow parts of herself.

In parenting, our intention is to be like the great sea. As we flow, effortlessly and fluidly, all things just flow with us and to us. When we make "mistakes", we see it and we look at our children as teachers who expose parts of us that are ready to be healed. Just because we grow up doesn't me we grow "whole". We often carry around wounded parts of ourselves, which get triggered by certain stages our children are in (typically the same "stage" at which we were wounded). Our children, then are our masters, if we let them, are pointing the way to our healing.

But, we cannot change it if we are not aware of it. Part of the process of become whole and living in peace (not pieces), is discovering what is *not* whole within us. Parenting does this oh-so-well.

We're often scared of our shadow self. Yet, it is just the part of us that gets revealed when there is enough light. Our backs are to the light and when we turn around and let the light wash over us, we can begin to heal. When we do this, our children become the beneficiaries of this because we are now parenting from a place that is light (and we tend to have a lot more compassion for them because we understand what they are going through).

When things come up for us, as we look at them with new eyes, we can ask ourselves, "Where is this coming from?" Or "Is this love talking or fear talking?" Are we afraid if we don't parent in a certain way (as we were parented), our children will turn out "bad"? Where in ourselves have we felt the same thing our child is going through (or done the same thing)? Did we "catch" our parents in lies or were they disrespectful to us and one another, and now we have zero tolerance when our children "seem" disrespectful (even if they are merely offering their opinion or want to challenge us on something)? Sometimes our views are skewed because we never had a "healthy" perspective from which to view a situation to begin with.

It's time for a new vantage point. When we are able to feel what we feel, which allows our hidden pains to be revealed, then we can finally deal with it and ultimately heal it. Feel it. Reveal it. Deal with it. Heal it.

Over and over again.

62

The Tao is the center of the Universe, a treasure for "good" and a refuge from "bad". Do not offer to help your child with your expertise, but teach him or her about the Tao. When we are one with the Tao, whatever we seek, we find. When we mess up, we are forgiven.

When our children are infants and very young, we are the center of their universe. We are where they take refuge. There are stages that children have "separation anxiety". They are so attached to their primary caregiver that they bury their little heads into their mommy or daddy's chest when a stranger even looks at them. It is easy to take on this role and forget that our job is to work ourselves out of a job. We are here to guide our children back towards themselves. We do this by showing them and teaching them the Tao, the Way and connecting them to their Ultimate Source.

When they are innately connected to this, wherever they turn, they are home. They have all the answers they seek within themselves. But, we are a society of outward seekers. There is always an expert to consult or someone outside of ourselves to reveal what is already there. I am not suggesting we do not seek guidance. It is wise to look to others further along the path, or those who have obtained great knowledge in a particular area. But, when it comes to life, love, peace, joy and true contentment, finding our way home and directing our children towards that path is an "inside job".

What does this look like? Whenever children inquire, ask them what they think first? Then, ask them about how they *feel*. Emotional Intelligence comes from the ability to check in with how we feel and to be able to "read" other people as well. A fun project is to take our children to the park or mall and play the "how are we connected game?" Ask them to see ways in which they are "the same" as others (they will typically find superficial things – hair color, glasses, boy or girl). But, what we're doing is fostering acceptance and a knowing that we are all connected. When we listen attentively to what they are saying and tap into what they are "feeling", we can help them to understand this and to create greater awareness of what it means to "know thyself".

63

Act without doing – effortless effort, manage without meddling, taste without tasting. Deal with the difficult, while it is still easy and accomplish big jobs by breaking them down into smaller steps. The Master never reaches for great, yet she always accomplishes great things. When she runs into obstacles, she stops and gives herself to it, she is o.k. with being uncomfortable, and therefore nothing is ever a problem.

This is the most difficult concept to understand in the Tao, in my opinion. It seems like such an oxymoron. How can you possibly "do without doing"? I think the answer lies in the words following this. When we deal with situations before they are problems, and when we break down what seems to be impossible into the possible, it is effortless. This is why parenting on purpose or consciously is so important. We create and foster a respectful, kind and unconditionally loving space while our children are still young (when it is easy), and when they grow into adolescence (more difficult) it is "effortless". The process is already established, the lines of communication are open, because we have taught our children that it is safe to tell the truth and that there is nothing we cannot handle about them.

We have shown them how to break down life into manageable steps, because we have done that ourselves. We do not "reach" (as in attach to results) because we are comfortable allowing things to unfold without controlling them or demanding they go a certain way. There are no problems, because every situation is an opportunity to learn and grow. When we operate from love, not fear, there is nothing we cannot look at or face. It doesn't mean we get it right all the time or the first time. But, what we're looking for is what wants to happen. Not what we want to *make* happen.

Being a conscious parent means we are continually awake and looking at what comes up within us. We aren't afraid of the dark places – we can say, "bring it on" because we know that we can't truly parent from a wounded place effectively. So, we deal with the "difficult" while it is easy, and when broken down, it is simply something that isn't working for us. We can release it and gravitate towards something greater.

We yell, we lose it, we "tap into" something painful for us. We reveal what caused this in the first place (we were yelled at about the same thing and never properly dealt with it, perhaps). We deal with it and heal it and often this looks like giving away what we did NOT get. What we needed was understanding, compassion, and love. What we most likely got was someone else's shame, guilt and pain. We can love ourselves and go back to our child, with a humble, "I'm sorry – that was *so* about me. Although I need you to clean up your room, I did not need to call you a 'slob' and tell you that you were lazy." With a warm hug of total acceptance and perhaps even a, "I was totally messy as a kid. It never felt good to feel like, because I was messy that I wasn't o.k. Everyone's messy sometimes. Let me help you break this down so it's not overwhelming."

The beauty of giving away what we want is that two people get to be healed. More importantly, we stop the cycle of wounding. Even more important is that we foster a loving, respectful, peaceful and safe environment.

Everyone wins in this space.

64

When something has deep roots, it is easy to nourish, when it is still new, easy to alter. Prevent trouble before it occurs, putting things in order before they exist. The journey of a thousand miles begins with a single step. When you hurry, you fail. When you try to hold on to something too tight, you lose it. Forcing something will ruin what was almost ripe. The Master allows things to take their own course, remaining calm – at the end as she was in the beginning. She has nothing; therefore, she cannot lose it. She is learning to "unlearn" and reminds her children of who they have always been. She tends to the Tao, which allows her to care for all things.

When our children get "grounded" (which the true meaning of the word is to return them to their Source), in the Truth of who they are it is easy to nourish them. While they are still fresh and new and growing, we can put things in order and truly prevent trouble by filling them up. You cannot give away what you do not possess. Many children today are walking around half-full and some even "broken". They bully because that is what is inside. Love when squeezed, squeezes out love. (You cannot get orange juice by squeezing an apple.) When children feel hurt, frustrated, disappointed, angry, they are "squeezed" and what inherently comes out is what we have nurtured and nourished them with.

When we set upon the path of the Tao, we take one step at a time and we do not hurry. We recognize that some things take time and we cannot force something to happen – we can allow what wants to happen and recognize that we cannot "lose" anything for we never possessed it in the first place. Our job, if we have one is to "unlearn" all the ways in which we are *not* relying on our Divine Nature and ways in which we do not connect to the Truth of who we are. When we do this, we are re-minding our children of who THEY are! When we re-mind them that they are perfect, made in the likeness and image of a Divine Creator that IS all things, they too can connect to this Presence to co-create love, joy, peace and experience their own greatness.

We begin to parent homeopathically. Parenting "homeopathically" to me is broken down like this: "Home-(to)Me- pathic. Pathic means a "way of being" (as in empathic – is a way of being and showing empathy). So, when we come home to ourselves "Me", we are able to show our children the

154

way "home" too. The journey of a thousand miles (our lifetime journey) begins right where we are. It is a single step in recognizing the Truth of who we are and continually parenting from this "home" and when we do that we resonate love which spills out to our child and washes over them. I have yet to find any problem that cannot be resolved with unconditional love. Jesus performed miracles from this place. A miracle is an adjustment to our thinking. It is an adjustment to what we think is right and true, to the alignment with what is.

65

Ancient Masters did not try to educate people, but they taught people to "not know". When people think they know everything, it is difficult to guide them, when they are open to "not knowing" they find their own way. The simple way is the clearest, content with an "ordinary life" you can show people back to their True Nature.

We cannot make someone learn anything. We can only provide opportunities for learning to occur. What is an environment conducive for learning? Think about how you learn? Most people do not learn when threatened or are motivated by fear. We tend to fight, take flight or stay frozen when we are in a state of fear. Yet, most of us still parent this way. There is an innate sense of fear that if we do not force our children to learn, they will somehow fail. What is ironic, it is the "forced learning" through fear, which is typically what holds all of us back from truly succeeding.

The simple way IS truly the clearest. When we are open to "not knowing" (how things will turn out, what our children will do when they grow up, or providing answers before our children even ask the questions), we are cultivating a safe, unconditionally loving environment from which our children can find their own way. They do anyway. It is what growing up is all about. We all rebel against what we are taught at some point, because we have to make it our own. How can we do that if we don't oppose it or at least look at it outside of ourselves? We "unlearn" someone else's experience and thrust upon learning so that we can digest it for ourselves.

It seems so simple. Yet, it is difficult. We must be open to the fact that we do not know. This then becomes all we truly need to know. Being open to not knowing, provides a blank slate-space. It gives permission to explore, question, and wrestle around with different ideas and thoughts. There is no right or wrong or a sense of judgment with the answers our child comes up with or even the questions. When you have a mind open to everything, yet unattached to anything, you have a mind ready to learn.

66

All streams flow to the sea because it is lower than they are. If you want to watch over people, put yourself below them and if you want to lead people, you must learn how to follow them. The Master is above people, yet they don't feel oppressed and she goes ahead of them, and they don't feel manipulated. She competes with no one.

Humility is a great quality in parenting. There is an assumption that as parents, we know it all. The truth is, we have merely had more time on this planet and more experience. We have not necessarily learned more (it all depends on how we took in our experiences), and most likely, we are more wounded. Yet, we often assume the stance with our children "above them" as if we have all the answers. Granted, we are in charge of their well-being and care, for they cannot fend for themselves. But, as they grow, are we cognizant of the fact that in order to "lead them", we need to follow them.

While doing therapy with my son, as he was in the throes of autism, it was very difficult to get him to come into my world. So, I had to join him in his. This looked like me continually following his lead. Where ever he would go and whatever he would do, I would follow. Sometimes this looked like me rocking with him. Sometimes this looked like me taking one of the hundreds of cars he would line up and holding it by my eyes for him to look at me. He would quickly snatch it back and put it back in line. But, for a moment, we "connected". Over a period of six months of continually doing this, I started to retrieve him and the connections became greater and longer. At 21, he is now "autistic-free" and indistinguishable from his peers and our connection is strong and beautiful.

But, I had to join him where he was first. As parents, we need to connect with our children where they are, not where we want them to be or think they should be. I had thought that I was not a big fan of rap, but when my son began to enjoy it, I asked him to share with me some of his favorites. I could truly enjoy it because this was a "window" into who he was. I actually found some songs I connected with (Tupac was one of the artists I "discovered" and Common, had some beautiful and profound things to say). I took a "learned belief" of mine (I did not like rap) and I allowed my son to teach me – to "unlearn" this.

When our children invite us into play, may we be open to them, may we be willing to "unlearn" some things we think we "know" and may we be humbled knowing that they, most likely have something they can teach us about ourselves!

67

Everyone says the Tao is great and beyond compare. But when you look inside yourself, it makes sense and the roots go deep. The Tao teaches simplicity, patience and compassion. Simple in what you think and what you do, you connect with your True Source. Patient with all beings, you flow with "what is". Compassionate with yourself, you are one with all that is.

This first is the essence of conscious parenting or C.P.S. (Conscious Parenting Strategies –which are Compassion, Patience, and Simplicity). Ironically, they are the same letters used for Child Protective Services.

When we are centered in the Tao, we are "rooted" in truth and connected to our Source. From this place, all things flow. It becomes effortless effort – simplicity at its best. You have endless patience (this does not mean that you don't ever "lose it" – it means that you spend more and more time in this space than not), and you have compassion (for yourself when you lose it! And for your child as they meander on and off the pathway).

This does not look like passive parenting. It is a very active and poised stance. With my 5 children, 4 of which are now "adults", I wish I could say that there was a "one size fits all" parenting style. I can say that over time, the underlying consistent factor in maintaining wholesome, respectful, honest and loving relationships with all of my children has been the concepts I am speaking about now. However, I have had to employ differing strategies with each of their different personalities.

I was the "perfect parent" until my youngest child came to me at age 36! I had read all the books, was working with children - I was an "expert". Ha! My daughter came to humble me and teach me many things. She did not respond as the other children had to the same techniques. She taught me to stand in my truth and that I couldn't waiver. She is intense, insatiable and came out of the womb talking! She spoke in paragraphs at age 1 (I kid you not!). I learned about setting healthy boundaries with her and that she needed to "bump" up against things to really get them.

When sitting in the "T.A.N.T. (Think A New Thought – taken from the concept of undoing a TANTrum) chair" – she reminded me (at the age of 18 months that I had forgotten to set the timer. In total exasperation (and not my best Mommy moment!) one night trying everything to get her to stay in bed (and she was oh-so-clever about her rationale...needing water, "growing pains", bathroom, her "Mommy tank was empty and she just needed 'this much' to fill her up!), I told her if she got out of bed one more time, I would take one of her stuffed animals away. To which she replied, "Well, which one?" She was weighing the consequences of how bad she wanted to get out of bad versus what she would lose! She was 5!

So, when I talk about employing this underlying current that flows throughout your parenting style, I understand that we still need to utilize specific strategies and techniques for teaching our children how to connect to Source but also live in human form. It is a precarious balance that will often challenge our sanity. But one in which we get to learn (sometimes in calm, sometimes in storm!) patience, compassion, and simplicity.

Although sometimes, this takes on the form of its opposite first!

68

All athletes want their opponent to be at their best. The best leader follows what the people want. They embody non-competition and do it in the spirit of play, like little children and in harmony with the Tao.

My favorite topic – Play! When we are allowing the Tao to flow effortlessly within us, we play very easily in, through and with life. When I feel connected, I play so easily with my life and it flows to my children. My youngest child has always had a difficult time separating at bedtime. It has been the stage of many dramas throughout her life. I have employed a multitude of strategies and of course, as a single mom, working full time, taking care of everyone and going to school full time, I had to make concerted efforts to employ patience, simplicity and compassion.

But, what I learned, is that playing with my daughter about this was the best strategy I could ever use. One night, after filling her "Mommy Tank" (or spending enough time in my mind that the tank HAD to be overflowing by now because I knew for sure I was close to empty!), she didn't want me to leave. So, I took her Hello Kitty stuffed toy and began speaking in an

English accent, that stated, "*I* am your mumsy now, and I shall be with you *all* through the night! Not to worry, dawling, you can hug me until morning!" She giggled with glee and went happily off to sleep as I crawled into bed. It took a mere 30 seconds to defuse the "I'm not going to bed" bomb that was about to explode in my face.

Playfulness is not the first place we go to. But, I really do believe it is our Essence. It is the place of authenticity and a place where we truly connect with our child. We have expectations of ourselves that we must be "serious, disciplined" and continually barking out commands and orders. When we play, our children get to see us in a new light – (literally) and for a moment connect with our Essence.

69

The generals say I would prefer to be the guest, than the host. This is called moving forward without going anywhere. There is nothing worse than underestimating the enemy. When two forces oppose each other, the victory goes to the one with compassion, and who knows how and when to concede.

So often in parenting we rush in and do for our children what they can do for themselves. We are quick to fix things that could possibly be worked out by our children (and an important lesson learned along the way). If we can wait for it, our children often surprise us. We misunderstand them when we fail to see the world the way they see it. We are bigger, have more experience and access to way more resources. They see things from the perspective of themselves and Now. When we are able to let go in the moment and in the struggle with the concept of being right, we have an opportunity to choose peace.

This is never more important than adolescence. We have spent many years raising our children at this point and are invested in "being right". We have an agenda. It's hard not to have one.

We have a way in which we like things done, perceptions about how our children should "behave", and what their grades should look like. There are parents who won't even let their child get their ears pierced or color their own hair! We want so much to "control" them and to make them our own that we forget that they are their own person and the more we resist, the more doors we open for rebellion.

When my daughter turned 18, she and a friend were going to go to one of those clubs 18-year-olds could go to. It was hilarious. They got all ready and as my daughter was leaving she asked me to "give her a curfew". I asked why, she said, "So I can break curfew." I said, "How about 1:00?" She said, "Make it 12:30!" Her friend was laughing hysterically! Well, she called me at midnight; they were at the In-N-Out drive thru on their way home. She hated it, "Can you believe they smoke there, mom? It was disgusting!" I joked and told her she was a terrible teen - she didn't even break curfew as she was home by 12:15!

She had nothing to rebel against. She had been allowed the freedom and flexibility in life to make choices for herself. She had learned throughout her life that there were consequences for her choices and this had built up her ability to see that *she* would "pay" for it one way or the other, not me.

70

The teachings of the Tao are easy to understand and put into practice, yet the mind will never grasp them. The teachings are older than the world. How can they be understood? You must look inside your heart.

The Tao, Life, or The Way is easy but when we intellectualize it, we will never understand it. How do we "do without doing"? It doesn't make any sense. And this is how we learn to live the Tao, by continually releasing that which "makes logical sense" and relying on the convictions of our hearts.

We do not "breathe" ourselves. We do not necessarily think of it, try to control it (or at least not all the time) and mostly remain unaware of our breath. Yet, we somehow manage to maintain life without any issue. This is the Tao. When we allow Life to breathe us, it is effortless. Doing this with parenting can be tricky because there is much we must "do" for our children. Therefore, we must remain conscious of what is ours to do, what needs to be released and continually checking in to determine if it is truly our problem, or is it our child's to own.

Mindful awareness is paying attention to the present moment. We do not do this often, as we are continually distracted. However, research states that the more we do it, the stronger we become at it. It is actually a skill we can develop and it is like a muscle, and when we practice mindful awareness by being fully present in the moment, it is like doing mental pushups for attention.

In spiritual practice, we often talk about meditation as a way to still our minds. We can make our lives a meditation, when we practice being aware. I like to say it is being in "awe" of where we are. We are *so* in the moment, that only what (or who) is in front of us gets our attention. When we begin practicing this with our children, they feel so honored to have us completely, you can actually see a difference in their behavior. Try spending 10 to 15 minutes each day in mindful awareness with your child. You shut off the "parenting" mode and just drop into "being with" your child and their beautiful essence. Your mind will not be able to grasp what your heart has been able to achieve.

71

To know you do not know is the highest awareness. When we think we know, we are flawed. However, when we recognize we are sick, we begin to move toward greater health. The Master is her own physician and has healed herself of all knowing. Therefore, she is truly whole.

You cannot change what you are not aware of. Becoming conscious of the ways in which we parent that are not healthy is the first step towards moving towards greater health. At first, we are moving away from something. Then, we move towards something.

We must first acknowledge that we "do not know" or that what we do know is incorrect. We relinquish what we think we know for "not knowing" and allowing. This looks like letting go of preconceived notions of who we think our child needs to be and our attachment to them showing up in a particular way. This is letting go of what others might think of our parenting skills if our child shows up "less than perfect". It is permission to be with what is and allow the freedom and flexibility to live out loud and outside of the lines.

It is recognizing the ways in which we ourselves have been wounded and look to heal what is coming up. If we look at our child and feel anxious about how they are showing up (or not), we evaluate the situation to see if this is "our stuff" or theirs. If they are showing up with bad grades, can we be autonomous and allow them to take responsibility for it (this does not mean we do not provide structure and support – we merely do not "attach" to their success as our own)? Did someone once tell us that we were not loveable for some reason? If our child doesn't get asked to the prom, does it illicit something from us that has not been healed?

Being a conscious parent is all about checking in continually to see what is living through us - our fears or love. It's simple. It's just not easy. We must be willing to give up what we think we know. We must be willing to let go of the pieces to truly live in peace.

72

The Master steps back so that people are not confused. She teaches without teaching so that people have nothing to learn.

Having "nothing to learn" simply means there is no agenda. The Master teacher does not need to teach anything. She does not need the child to learn anything. She steps back out of the mess so that she is not muddying the waters. It is not hers to do. When her child is in conflict, she steps back so that she is not inserting her will in the situation. She is clear when it is hers to intervene. She is clear when her child is learning without her needing to "teach".

The best lessons our children learn are the ones in which we are out of the way. When we are "in the way", instead of getting the lesson, they get mad at us and blame us for the way things went. They leave their coat at home when we have always rescued them or reminded them or "I told you so'ed" them. If we mention, "It is cold out. You might need a jacket today." (Information they do not have). If they leave the jacket at home, they learn. If we fight over the jacket, we have taught them not to listen to themselves. They will learn more about being prepared when they spend one recess being cold then they ever will with us hounding them to "remember your jacket". This works with homework, forgotten lunches, and getting out of bed in the morning.

It is interesting as parents; we have issues with allowing our children to learn through natural consequences. Yet, we have no issue punishing them relentlessly, yelling at them and shaming them. Allowing our children to suffer life consequences (going to bed hungry because they don't like what we are serving and refuse to eat it) is difficult for us. Yet, think of the ways in which you have learned life. We learn when it matters. It won't "matter" to our child if we are taking responsibility for them (continually bringing them their lunches, putting their homework in their backpacks – long past the time that they should be doing it themselves). We teach without teaching by stepping back and letting life do the teaching.

73

The Tao is at peace with whatever happens and can answer all of life's problems without saying a word and arrives without being asked and gets things done without a plan. The net is vast and loose, yet nothing slips through it.

When we are at ease, there is nothing that comes to us that we are for or against. It just is. We can allow all things because we are not attached to a "story" about it. Our child brings home bad grades – we ask ourselves, "What is my story about this?" When we relinquish the story, we are able to answer without saying a word. We move into action. First, we look and see, "What is my child trying to tell me?" All behavior is a language, so we move towards interpretation. Sometimes, it is as simple as they need help with a subject – they aren't getting it. When we are not attached to a story, we move with ease, provide support (if we can and if not, we get a tutor or help from the teacher). If there is a bigger issue (either a learning disorder), we are again, not attached to a story (my child is lazy), and we can move towards appropriate action.

If the issue is, our child is struggling in another area of their lives (they don't have friends, a recent divorce, a loss, or low self-esteem), by being unattached to the "result" (bad grades), we can look deeper at how we can support our child. When we accept all things, it does not mean we leave them this way. It just means we see them clearly without a "story" (ours or someone else's) so that we can interpret correctly what is going on and move lovingly and with ease and grace towards an appropriate solution.

What if your child is always dawdling or late? What story have you created? Sometimes, we are not even conscious of the fact that we have a story. We just know that it irritates us and is a point of contention between us and our child. When we drop the story, we look and ask ourselves, "Is my child trying to tell me something?" Maybe their clock is set a little slower and they are reminding us to slow down and accept them the way they are. Or maybe they are trying to gain some control of their hurried life. Maybe they are resisting something. We don't know if we already "know" because we are not open to anything other than what we have decided it is. When we are open and at ease, we allow another idea or solution to be brought in by the Tao, one that is in alignment with Truth and not just a "story".

Conscious parenting is a blanket that covers our entire child with breathable skin and has enough openings for them to grow and learn on their own. It provides a safety net where they are continually loved and accepted, yet free to roam about, learn and discover their world and themselves.

We want to cover them. Not smother them.

74

When you realize that things are constantly changing, you stop trying to hold onto them. If you aren't afraid of losing anything, there is nothing you cannot do. Trying to control the future is like trying to take the Master Carpenter's place. When you mess with the Master Carpenter's tools, most likely you might hurt yourself.

We love the concept of impermanence. We love the idea that "this is it". We want to eradicate messes, unacceptable behaviors, even signs of life's process permanently. We want to look forever young, have a definitive answer about life's big questions and know for sure, once and for all that everything is o.k.

The truth is – everything is continually changing and although everything will always be o.k. in the end (and if it's not o.k., it is not the end!), it is so difficult to relinquish our grip on the impermanence.

Erma Bombeck once said, "Trying to clean a house while the kids are still young is like trying to shovel the sidewalk before it snows." We laugh, but how often do we "hold onto" messes as if they were not normal? *Life* is messy, creation is messy (you can't make an omelet without cracking some eggs).

And although we've gotten better about tolerating creative messes (such as art projects, sleepovers and our kids making cookies), we still struggle with the "messes" they make learning about life. Life is messy and there is no permanent solution to that. Yet, how often when our children struggle with life, do we want to start shoveling the sidewalk? Our fears (of being inadequate, not doing enough, not being enough, of what other people might think of us, that our children will somehow turn out to be one of "those kids"), keep us messing with the Master Carpenter's tools – and very often we end up cutting ourselves – and our children in the process.

When we are able to reveal these fears, deal with them and consciously choose to operate from a place of love, we make different decisions and choices. We "allow" the mess of our child figuring out life because first of all, we believe in their inherent ability to figure it out, and secondly, we also trust life. We trust the Tao that flows in and through all things to love up our child and provide the same wisdom and guidance that we ourselves receive when we need it.

We stop being afraid of losing anything, because we become aware that anything that can be lost is not part of our True Essence.

75

Act for the children's benefit. Trust them and let them Be.

If you spend enough time with children what you discover is first of all, they are incredibly honest and perceptive. They see (and speak into) that which most of us try hard not to acknowledge – things like injustices, unkindness or simple truths. Another thing you notice is that up until a certain age, there is a belief that anything is possible and that they truly see the "good" in all things.

If we were to trust this and leave them alone with this, we might see a lot more people grow up believing in the good, and that they are here for a purpose and can do anything that their soul is nudging them to do. If we were to truly act for their benefit, we would spend a lot more of our efforts protecting their innocence and nurturing their inherent connection to their Divine Essence.

We offer wisdom and guidance by way of how we ourselves live our life. Do we continually complain about lack – lack of money, lack of love, lack of time, lack of friends? Do we complain about our job, our spouse, our lives? Are we yelling at the clerk at the store or screaming profanities to the driver who cut us off? Or are we nurturing and caring to all we encounter? Are we patience and grateful and filled with unrelenting Joy? When we are squeezed, what comes out?

I guarantee, that is exactly the "juice" that our children are drinking in. We can "tell" them how to live. We can punish them for the ways in which they are not measuring up to what we have required. But at the end of the day, when we "act" for their benefit, it is the stage of our lives that we play on that they are watching and learning from.

If we get very real about our own process, there is very little we need do. For who we *are* will speak so loudly to our children that they won't even need to listen to what we say.

76

We are all born soft and supple. When we die, we are hard and stiff. Therefore, when we are stiff and inflexible, we are practicing death. When we are soft and yielding, we are practicing life. That which is hard and stiff breaks, that which is soft and supple overcomes.

When babies are born, their brain is the only organ not fully formed. It is supple, soft and available to take in new information – to learn and to grow. They download a lot of information in the first few years. Being open to learn, there is so much to take in. Children learn to dance before they even know that there is anything that is *not* music. They are open, alive, and willing to believe anything. This is why they have a difficult time understanding the difference between what is "real" and what is "pretend".

As we grow, we begin to die a little at a time and can become very stiff, hard, and rigid in our thinking. We begin to believe there is only one way to do something and it is usually our way. My children have taught me numerous times a different (and more efficient way) of doing things. I used to think they were lazy. Yet, I softened to understand that they were very efficient and were wise in conserving their energies for activities they enjoyed. They were able to accomplish the same task with a more efficient system.

When I find myself resisting change with my parenting or my children, I try to open up and ask myself if I am open to life or have I hardened in some way that is not serving me? My son was in his first year of college. I was very "invested" as we had worked very hard to overcome his diagnosis of autism and this was his first "solo flight". He had a major project due and waited until the last minute to do it. This is not how I function and I was having a moment of being stiff and inflexible. I let go and recognized this was not "my problem" and simply showed my support by acknowledging he was able to do anything he set his mind to. He rocked it and got a 100%. His mind was streamlined and efficient in doing this all at once.

At some point, since we're working ourselves out of a job, we must let go and give in to life and allow our child to do the same. Learning that their way might look different than ours, gives us an opportunity to be supple and soft. We can still suggest and give ideas. But, ultimately, they learn how to do life by ... doing life.

There simply is no other way.

77

The Tao is like a bow that bends, that adjusts too much and not enough to achieve perfect balance. It takes from too much and gives to not enough.

When we parent with the Tao, we bend and move like branches blown by the wind. We can adjust automatically with too much or not enough because we maintain balance. The Tao is all about maintaining the middle way. So often we are parenting "too much" or not enough. It is all about living life in balance and allowing life to teach our children how to live, while we provide a mirror for their True Essence.

We cannot give away what we do not have, though. If we are not connected to our True Selves, we are going to struggle with pointing our children to this True Self. We find this space by finding out first what it is "not". It is not the "idea" we have of ourselves or the many faces we wear. It is not our age, dress size, income level, education, roles we play (mother, father, daughter, son, brother, sister, lover, best friend), nor is it the wounded parts of ourselves that continually tell us that we are not enough.

The "unlearning" must come first. We have to let go of what we think we know about who we are to go back to our Original Self that is whole and perfect. We came in that way and the process of life has kicked that True Self to the curb. By becoming conscious of this, we do not pass on this Spiritual Abuse to our children.

But, we must dig deep enough to see what we are not looking at that might be clouding how we view our children. Our children tend to reflect back to us the Truth and we often have a hard time reconciling this with what we have "swallowed" as the truth about ourselves.

We cannot accept in them what we have rejected in ourselves. We cannot excavate the wholeness within our children if we are not aware of it within ourselves. To do this, we must first re-negotiate a new agreement with ourselves and what we believe the Truth to be.

78

Nothing in the world is as soft and yielding as water. Nothing surpasses it for softening the hard and inflexible. The soft overcomes the hard; the gentle overcomes the rigid. We all know this, but few of us practice this. Because she has given up helping people, she is people's greatest helper.

Water seeks its own level and with consistency, patience and perseverance, overcomes and transforms even the rockiest of terrain. When we are soft and yielding, we can go anywhere. We can flow into the nooks and crannies of our children's lives, because we are truly liquid. When we draw hard lines (usually based on fear) with our children, we break (or we end up breaking them).

The conundrum with parenting is precariously balancing the human and the spirit. Our children are learning to become human and need specific guidelines for what this looks like. Their brains are growing and developing, and they are uploading a lot of information in the first few formative years. They need guidance and they need to hear "no", understand it, assimilate it, repeat it back and integrate so that they are able to say "no" to dangers and things that do not serve them throughout their lives.

While at the same time, we want to nurture their innate ability to soar. We want them to practice making healthy choices, learn to live with the consequences, be connected to their True Self and know that they are perfect and whole just as they were created!

When we "help" it is from the stance of breaking down tasks into manageable steps – not doing it for them. Given our lifestyles, many of our children today do not have a lot of chores or responsibilities at home. (Very few kids have to get up and milk the cows or help with the farm anymore before going to school.) As I work with families with teens, there are many who do not know how to do laundry, make a meal, set a budget (let alone stick with one), or even fill out basic paperwork for job applications or college. In our desire to be "good parents", we often handicap our children by doing for them what they can do for themselves.

As we begin to parent consciously, we look at what we are doing and ask ourselves, "Is this my child's to do?" If so, "How can I facilitate them doing it?" Accomplishments fuel self-efficacy, which is necessary for a healthy self-esteem. Self–

efficacy states, "No matter what, I can do this." It is a belief in one's abilities. In order to acquire this, children need opportunities to exercise their abilities.

We help them when we stop helping them so much.

79 ,

The Wise woman takes care of her own mistakes and does not require payment from others. Heaven knows no favorites but supports only the good.

When we take responsibility for what is ours and allow our children to do the same, punishment is unnecessary. Natural consequences replace punishment in that we have no agenda. We have no need to impart our will on our children and we allow life to do the teaching. We are there, with compassion, patience and simplicity, "soft as water" to flow in where our wisdom and guidance provide support, not a lecture.

We do not need "payment" when we are right. We allow our child to learn from their mistakes by removing ourselves from the problem. We support the "good" in them without favoring one outcome or another.

When we are living in the Tao, we see the good in our children and we step back to ask, "What is my child trying to communicate with this (missed) behavior?"

We also forgive ourselves for the ways in which we haven't always parented consciously. We let go of the things that we have done along the way that have "muddied" the waters. We become clear in this moment, relinquish the past, say our "sorries", where necessary and move on.

We can only live in this moment and we take responsibility for our mistakes by not continuing to do the same thing.

My eldest daughter has had the tendency to accumulate dishes in her room and then brings them all down at once. If the dishwasher is full, she places on the counter. Most often, she will put them in the dishwasher, when it is unloaded. However, sometimes, it is so frustrating to see them there – just taunting me (my story, of course!). One day, I came down and all I could see was the messiness. I didn't see her, but the mess. I launched on her about the mess. Later, I realized, it was my own "messy" life at the moment that was creating the chaos. It was not the kitchen and it was definitely not all *her* mess. I went down and articulated this to my daughter, with an apology. Later, she cleaned up the kitchen without my even asking (her mess and everyone else's). When we take responsibility for our own mistakes, we give others permission to do the same and self-correct. Isn't this what the process of life is all about?

80

Let the people return to tying knots and using them and to savor their food, admire their clothes, content in their homes, and happy in their customs.

As we parent consciously, we return to simplicity. We go back to happy customs. We have become a society of so much busyness, that even when we are still, we are "active" (checking Facebook updates while in a waiting room, reading emails while out to dinner, texting one friend, while in the presence of another). We do this and we teach our children to do this. We are not "savoring" moments with our children, because we are not usually fully present.

Returning to contentment looks like "savoring food" – having dinner together, where we share our days, what happened, what was good, and what was difficult. We have simple rituals at tuck-in with a favorite story, or family game night or family movie night. It looks like being fully present, "unplugging" and plugging into one another – wholly and fully.

Our children are not wanting for more gadgets, electronics or phone apps. They are hungering for a "parent app" that connects them deeply and fully to their Divine Essence.

Research shows us that for the first few years we unquestionably absorb the beliefs of others. It is not for many years that we actually acquire the ability to question these beliefs. The brain is stubborn in that once these original beliefs are established; it has a hard time accepting opposing beliefs. Research shows how powerful beliefs can be. With over 6 billion differing belief systems, there is much to sift through and we all cling to certain beliefs to get us through the day.

When we settle into being content and happy, we might negotiate a change in our belief system that would support this differing style of parenting. Although our brains might resist this notion at first, if we return to the simplicity of it all, it begins to make sense and we are able to slowly relinquish the beliefs that are keeping us from authentically connecting with our child.

81

Words that speak truth are not necessarily "beautiful" and flattering words are not necessarily true. When you do "good" there is no need to debate. Those who know, need not prove their point. The more wise ones give, the more they get. The Tao does not harm – does not force and therefore all wish to follow it.

We spend a lot of time "talking" to our kids and sometimes the words we speak are unnecessary. When we parent consciously, we are aware that our words are powerful and are our "wands" – as we speak it, so it is. When we are continually telling our children what they are (smart, dumb, lazy, pretty etc.) our words are not necessarily "true" but our children believe them, which makes them true for our child. When we parent from fear, we might often worry that the teenagers sitting on the couch watching TV. for hours on end is, in fact, lazy. Or what is usually the case, is someone once told us that about ourselves and we are carrying that wound into the now.

When we see, foster and nourish the good inside our children, we do not need to debate. We know their inherent goodness is there, and we speak to that. We do not force what we think needs to happen, we accept them where they are at and allow the Truth to speak through us which is only loving-kindness and that which nourishes and builds up. There is nothing to prove and we don't need to be "right".

Our children are processing their world the best they know how to. Our brains are wired to be efficient, so when there is too much to take in, our brains will identify what it believes to be significant and throw out the rest. Well, imagine what is "significant" for a child versus what is significant for an adult. With this process, important information can be eliminated, especially when evaluating new experiences. Our children are continually doing this, so it makes sense that things get "lost" in their brain along the way. But, we understand this and do no harm and do not need to prove any point.

Epilogue

As we allow the Tao to flow through us, we settle into conscious parenting with ease and grace. We challenge the long-held beliefs, thoughts and feelings and allow ourselves to *be* lived, accepting what "is" and continually returning to the space that resides within that is unconditionally loving, filled with relentless joy, and unending peace.

This is why it is called The Way. It points us back to our Original Selves and we can come home.

When we come home to ourselves, we become a safe and sacred place for our child to gravitate to and then to propel from to find their own Way.

About The Author

Dr. Lisa Smith was born and raised in Ohio but moved to Phoenix, AZ twenty-three years ago where she currently resides with 4 of her 5 children. When Lisa's son was diagnosed with autism at age 3 ½ she began a passionate quest comprised of research, education and hands-on experience and she created a program that ultimately led to the remediation of her son's autism. Now, at age 21, he is considered indistinguishable from his peers! She has taken this life-learning, coupled with a Master's Degree in Child and Adolescent Developmental Psychology, a Master's and Doctorate in Metaphysics and Transpersonal Counseling, certification in Family Effectiveness Training, and as a Neurodevelopmentalist to assist other families. Her life mission is to share this eclectic experience and knowledge to help parents to parent consciously or "on purpose". She works with families of all kinds to create a business model for parenting with a program known as ESP (Effective Strategies for Parenting) and teaches CPS (Conscious Parenting Strategies) for effective parenting. Lisa believes that all behavior is a language and teaches parents to interpret this language. She also believes that effective strategies must incorporate the child's mind, body and spirit to create strong efficacy and self-esteem. These integrated practices create a whole child who is "monster-proof" for life!

Lisa hosts workshops around the country, has authored four books and is available for private consultation.

Other Books By Dr. Lisa M. Smith

Do Not, I Say DO NOT Think of a Pink Elephant

Mommy, What Does Love Look Like?

My Brother has Oddism: A Child's Misinterpretation of the Diagnosis of Autism

Dear Kenton, Can You Hear Me? Love, Mommy

Printed in Great Britain
by Amazon